# HEAVEN'S RAGE
## Childhood, Survival
## and
## Crossing the Gender Line

Leslie Tate

**TSL Publications**

First published in Great Britain in 2016
By TSL Publications, Rickmansworth

Copyright © 2016 Leslie Tate

ISBN / 978-1-911070-48-1

To

Frieda, Chris and Penny

# Acknowledgements

Thank you to my dear wife Sue Hampton who has read this book with love and close attention, helping me to correct and improve everything in it.

Thank you to two gifted friends: Sheelagh Frew Crane for her wonderful portrait of me, and Mark Crane for taking that portrait and turning it into a beautiful cover design.

Thank you to the patient, skilled Anne at TSL for her faith in this book and her help and support in producing it.

Thank you to all my willing reviewers for taking the time to read and comment on sections of the book.

*The aim of writing is to make every word count. As in jazz or a great speech what appears to be improvised comes out of years of practice.*

*Art and life are unlike twins.*

*In searching for the exact word for every experience the writer discovers the hidden inner self, waiting to be heard.*

# 1st MOVEMENT

# FOLLOW YOUR STAR

## What readers said about:
*Tales of John Barleycorn*
*Let's Face the Music*
and
*The Art of Gardens*

A new book by Leslie Tate is not just a literary event, it's a becoming-more-human event. In *Heaven's Rage*, he writes brilliantly about alcoholism, music, gardening, exploring complex identity, surviving and thriving. Any writer who can discuss addiction, Muddy Waters and gardening in the same frank, witty, and knowledgeable volume will find a place on my kitchen and bedside table.

The opening chapter on alcoholism offers an insider's view on recognizing the problem and coping with it; it is worth the price of admission. I am guessing we all know someone who could benefit from this well-written collection. Memoir, yes, but not private; personal, yes, but fascinating, entertaining, and useful to general readers and literature students alike. A companion for those who are crossing gender lines and need an intelligent, compassionate guide by their side. A gift for those who treasure the English language and value a good read!
– *Dr. Marilyn Kallet, Nancy Moore Goslee Professor of English, Author of 17 books, including The Love That Moves Me, poetry from Black Widow Press.*

Here is an eclectic mix of autobiography, fiction, scientific research, poetry and philosophy. *Tales of John Barleycorn* is a very honest self-analysis of both alcoholism and abstinence showing how these two opposites can be inhibiting or liberating in equal measure. *Let's Face the Music* examines the idea of music as a universal language. What I find most fascinating is the proven healing effects of nature explored in *The Art of Gardens*. Here, the author provides us with results of medical studies, a sensual and evocative walk

through beautiful gardens, a sensitive poem about Hidcote and a short extract from a novel. The garden becomes real, imaginary and a metaphor — and nature is both life-enhancing and energising. And who wouldn't want to 'taste life twice, in the moment and in retrospect'?
— *Mary Biddington, Artist and Photographer.*

In these three pieces Leslie Tate writes sensitively about:
♪ The addict's journey as a Homerian epic. Will the petty and obsessive transgressions win (tanking up in the kitchen while making coq-au-vin), or will the soul's truthfulness (I want to be a writer, an honest artist) prevail?
♪ Music as an atavistic yet subtle passion that alerts the boy Leslie to the rhythms of his own mind.
♪ Gardens that bring people close to nature — linking the words of a poem, the paragraphs of a novel, and the delicate vicissitudes of a marital relationship.
These are matters Leslie Tate makes us care about.
— *Philippa Jones, Lecturer Digital Media, University of Hertfordshire.*

*Tales of John Barleycorn* shows how social drinkers misunderstand the alcoholic's conscious choice of sobriety. *Let's Face the Music* beautifully explores the coming-of-age process, capturing its contradictory feelings. *The Art of Gardens* examines the meaning of the garden to the human psyche and its restorative effect on intelligence and the body. A good read for everyone.
— *Suzanne Watts, Communications Consultant.*

I loved reading these. *Tales of John Barleycorn* was a relentless portrayal of the insidious effects of alcohol on an addictive personality and *The Art of Gardens* was full of surprises! I was fascinated by the interactions between people — both real and fictional — and the setting; entranced by the beautifully descriptive prose.
— *Elizabeth J. Walker, Teacher and Author of The Resilience Handbook.*

# TALES OF JOHN BARLEYCORN

I'm an alcoholic. When I tell people at parties, they usually don't know what to say. Some smile as if they already knew; others look confused or worried. Often there's a pause while they work out their reply. 'OK,' they're thinking, 'what do I do next?' or they're wondering whether I'm joking. Occasionally they say something like, 'Oh, but you're all right with drink *now*?' and offer me a glass. That's when I explain that alcoholism doesn't go away, adding that though I haven't indulged for twenty years, when I did one Christmas it soon escalated. Even after that there are still a few who won't take no for an answer — probably first-stage alcoholics themselves — but for most people what they find odd is the idea of total abstinence. To them, saying no to pleasure just isn't done. It has a nonconformist edge to it, a kind of disrespect for 'do as I do' and playing by the rules. You can almost hear them asking each other, 'Well, would *you* say no to a drink?' Of course they're all perfectly well-intentioned, but in a materialist age you grab what you can get, calling it your right to party. Anyone who doesn't is an oddball who needs careful watching. Because to step out of line seems dangerous to those who fear the cold sober eye of judgement when they're at their worst.

But for me renunciation is freedom. It keeps me inside a charmed circle and out of harm's way. When I drank I knew no limits. It was as self-punishing as any high-performance sport. And I thrived on its highs and lows because they made me feel alive. I had my dream, an unreal bubble surrounding me, and as long as I remained in there I was important.

In fact I was more of a spectator, watching myself going under. When I looked in the mirror I could see I'd changed. My face had hardened in a way that wasn't obvious to the world. It had a subtle mask-like quality, a defensive stillness, like a patient after an operation. There were other changes too, mostly physical:

♪  I had what they call marmalade eyes.
♪  My hands shook slightly when they came close to a glass.
♪  I drank too quickly, all evening, and sometimes from the bottle.
♪  In the morning my body ached all over.
♪  Occasionally, I wet myself.
Like many addicts, I developed defensive strategies. So I hid my empty

bottles or added water to the dregs to give the impression that I'd hardly touched a drop. I looked up recipes such as coq au vin and chicken marsala because they allowed me to have shots in the kitchen without being seen. And I brewed my own, filling the cellar with brown popping mixtures in bell jars and vats.

Drink kept me busy. To ensure my supplies, I bought in fermentation kits and memorised the opening times of all the local 'offies'. When shopping, I studied the labels to get my fix of alcohol, calculating proof against price. I developed a keen interest in wine with meals, celebrating birthdays and going out to parties — where I'd lurk in corners, 'tanking up'. If challenged, I lied about how much I'd had, or I'd turn it back on my first wife, telling her she was over-reacting and being bossy. My line was that I would handle it — not now but soon, when I was ready. The unspoken corollary was, 'don't bother me, I'm too busy living'.

In fact I used a long list of mental evasions to keep the truth from myself. So the voice in my head was busy saying things like:

*You know you can change, tomorrow will be different.*

*Just remember Blake, 'the road of excess leads to the palace of wisdom'.*

*Someday you'll write it all up, as a warning to others.*

At other times I saw it as a mission, exploring the places other people didn't dare go. On that journey I'd a secret belief that my luck would hold and I'd find a way through. Recalling my childhood, I pictured myself hiding in bushes and crawling unseen behind back garden fences. But the mornings-after were different. Words like *damaged* and *broken* filled my head. I'd been foolish, I'd lost my way, and now I feared there'd be no turning back. I was also afraid because I couldn't seem to stop and the threat of running dry was an ever-present danger — and what would I do if I ran out? It would be like stepping into darkness without a torch. In any case, I told myself, quoting Keats, this was my 'vale of soul-making'. So I came to accept drink as a calling, and I fantasised about living wild and running in the woods, about rescue, rebirth and personal greatness ...

A study by Alan R. Lang[1] found that the addictive personality, 'values nonconformity, with a corresponding weak commitment to socially valued goals for achievement'. In my case, the thing I really valued was ruled out by my parents. They wanted me to be practical, to study hard, go to

---

[1] Lang, Alan R. (1983). "Addictive Personality: A Viable Construct?". In Levison, Peter K.; Gerstein, Dean R.; Maloff, Deborah R. Commonalities in Substance Abuse and Habitual Behavior. Lexington Books. pp. 157–236. ISBN 978-0-669-06293-9. Lay summary — The New York Times (January 18, 1983).

Oxbridge and get a top job. I don't think it occurred to them that I might have other plans — and the power of their opinions kept me quiet. I knew if I said I wanted to be a poet they'd tell me flatly that was impossible. In their world, you had to get real. Everyone needed money, so it was *head down, lad, and prepare for life.*

Later, as a teacher, I found myself drifting, feeling I was wasted. Although I could handle the job, for me it wasn't enough. Every day I'd go through the motions, feeling blocked, while struggling not to show it. I'd a passion inside, an urge to do something big and rash and final — and the drink was how I coped. In terms of A.R. Lang's formula I had a different set of values and I couldn't connect.

Most addictions develop slowly. Looking back we search for a trigger, a critical moment where something set it off. But the truth is it's more about habit than chance, and regular drinking easily gets out of hand. In my case, it crept up on me, starting with 'sampling' different drinks, moving on to 'one more for the road' ending with 'finishing the bottle'. It never reached the stage of drinking in the morning or at work, but in the evening I charged up steadily from the moment I got home. I'd put away four bottles of wine, maybe some cider as well. If they were homemade I could just about handle it, drinking water to head off the hangover, but shop-bought was different. Beginning in my gut, the numbness would spread, filling my body and stiffening my mouth as if I'd been to the dentist. I was inside a glow, an invisible blur that softened everything. There was a screen between me and life: I was safe; I was oblivious. And I experienced my thoughts at one remove, out there at a distance, floating in the room. If you'd asked me to walk in a straight line, I couldn't have done it. I didn't see pink elephants but my habit had taken over and the song in my head was *John Barleycorn Must Die.*[2]

For a long time I didn't want it to end. I made promises, broke them, made them again, stayed dry for a few days then binged all weekend. I tried cutting down, pacing my intake or using smaller glasses, but my habit returned — all the more extreme for being denied. I didn't change personality because of the drink but I was always on the lookout for my next

--------

[2] Robert Burns's ballad *John Barleycorn Must Die* begins:
There was three kings into the east,
Three kings both great and high,
And they hae sworn a solemn oath
John Barleycorn should die.
        See end of chapter for Steve Winwood's version.

opportunity — and I learned to deceive, because addiction and lies are close bedfellows. To give a few examples:

♪ I drank unseen on landings and behind locked doors.
♪ When my wife went out I charged up to the limit then drank black coffee until she got home.
♪ I lied about how much I'd spent and where I'd been.
♪ With guests I smiled and passed myself off as sober.
♪ When I went to AA I objected to the 'confessionals' and the twelve steps. The truth was I was afraid of giving up.

So how did I stop?

It wasn't through will power; I'd tried that and failed more than once. I didn't take advice or go into rehab and although I'd come out as trans, I kept on drinking. But a moment arrived when I realised what I was doing — not just in theory but as it actually touched me, on the inside. I'd become my own prisoner, the man passed over who locks himself away. Looked at socially, I was sailing through; relative to my ambition, my life was on the rocks. And the key was my refusal. As a writer and a poet, I thought I couldn't do it. And rather than risk failure, I'd decided to opt out and not try at all.

That moment of insight turned things around. I made a declaration, first to my wife but later to friends, using the A word and asking them, if they saw me drinking, to call me out. It stopped me. Because what I'd said, I'd said: I'd made my statement and burnt my bridges. And to keep my resolution, and by way of reparation, I promised myself that one day I'd write it down ...

And now, going back to that moment when I'm offered a drink, I hear myself explaining, maybe quietly in a place inside myself, that it's not about denial or spoiling other people's fun. Because I'm happy being sober. But there's always that voice inside telling me it's OK and why not try it, that this time it won't matter. The voice sounds calm and questions everything. It's the voice of the lush, the long-term dipso, the man who can't cope. He's asking me to listen, telling me he's hurt, pushing to be heard. But I know how to handle him, listening patiently while refusing to be drawn. And whatever he says, I won't be tempted ...

---

[2] Note continued ...

*Steve Winwood*'s version appears on the eponymous 1971 album by *Traffic*:

### John Barleycorn (Must Die)

There were three men came out of the west, their fortunes for to try
And these three men made a solemn vow
John Barleycorn must die
They've plowed, they've sown, they've harrowed him in
Threw clods upon his head
And these three men made a solemn vow
John Barleycorn was dead

They've let him lie for a very long time, 'til the rains from heaven did fall
And little Sir John sprung up his head and so amazed them all
They've let him stand 'til Midsummer's Day 'til he looked both pale and wan
And little Sir John's grown a long long beard and so become a man
They've hired men with their scythes so sharp to cut him off at the knee
They've rolled him and tied him by the way, serving him most barbarously
They've hired men with their sharp pitchforks who've pricked him to the heart
And the loader he has served him worse than that
For he's bound him to the cart

They've wheeled him around and around a field 'til they came onto a pond
And there they made a solemn oath on poor John Barleycorn
They've hired men with their crabtree sticks to cut him skin from bone
And the miller he has served him worse than that
For he's ground him between two stones
And little Sir John and the nut brown bowl and his brandy in the glass
And little Sir John and the nut brown bowl proved the strongest man at last
The huntsman he can't hunt the fox nor so loudly to blow his horn
And the tinker he can't mend kettle or pots without a little barleycorn.

# LET'S FACE THE MUSIC

*Music expresses that which cannot be said and on which it is impossible to be silent*
— Victor Hugo

*Without music, life would be a mistake*
— Friedrich Nietzsche

*Music is the best means we have of digesting time*
— Igor Stravinsky

*Music, in performance, is a type of sculpture. The air in the performance is sculpted into something*
— Frank Zappa

Schopenhauer believed that, 'Aesthetic pleasure in the beautiful consists, to a large extent, in the fact that, when we enter the state of pure contemplation, we are raised for the moment above all willing, above all desires and cares; we are, so to speak, rid of ourselves'.[1]

When I was young, I wanted to live at that level all the time, but it only really happened when I tried. Listening I'd push myself, rising with the highs, descending with the lows and straining my feelings to follow every note. When my father played Beethoven I'd angle my head back on the sofa while he conducted an imaginary orchestra. Like him, I wanted to enter into the spirit of the music as deeply as I could. So I worked on being 'carried away', developing the kind of self-consciously abandoned behaviour that Schopenhauer says 'demands a complete forgetting of our own person'.[1] After my father's death I wrote an elegy about the effort that went into it.

---

1 Schopenhauer, The World as Will and Representation vol. I.

## His Master's Voice

*Hush.* My mind in his: eyes closed, head back on sofa,
then concert-lifted, sustained through sound,
pondering on greatness in The Eroica. *Listen.* The eternals come up.
Studying the sleeve notes in the dark-lined room
to work on response, on knowing abandon,
guarded and wild to force out soul.

*Shhh.* Not the man but his greatness.
Ambition concealed behind thick black glasses,
hair-roots, recessions and shadows from the lamp.
His genius in hiding, sunken, cornered,
driven below thought, as vinyl oblivion eddies to a storm.

*Sforzando.* His mind: and mine. Now down, now up, the music builds
to overwrought dramas, needlings and impossibles
and last-chance campaigns. The elements grow large.
His importance, still with me, proud and given, overstrains life.
Experts in this, we have it all by heart.

*Hush.* That's him. Admiring, I sit tight. The house lights dim.
I imagine him there, poised and intent, with baton lifted,
tapping to begin. A cough, a shuffle, the rustle of a programme,
and the absolute begins. It swells against the heart
through abstracts of heroism to greatness still to come.
The everlasting calls: dark and stirring, it overwhelms sense.
Surely they must hear? The lift and resonance, the architectural truth.
And the final recognition as, high up in darkness, big-souled, thoughtful,
his stillness calls me from somewhere in the night

*ppp.*

There were other elevated moments with music. When I sang at Christmas in front of my family the notes seemed to fill the room. I was my performer-self: charming, bashful and yet 'out of my skin'. Although my pieces were short — a few well-known carols accompanied on piano by my grandmother — I was entranced by their beauty and gave myself up to them.

As I grew older I developed my own musical tastes — or obsessions — moving from the *1812 Overture* to *Pictures at an Exhibition, Manfred* and the *Symphonie Fantastique*. I listened to these pieces as drama, seeing them as film scenes running in my head. As my interests widened I 'discovered' composers like Alkan and Scriabin, beat time to *Boléro* and *The Planets*, and cast myself as Horowitz or Cziffra performing Liszt.

My tastes suddenly changed when I discovered pop music. Klemperer and Rubinstein gave way to Billy Fury and The Four Seasons. It was my Radio Luxembourg phase, listening surreptitiously to a turned-down transistor radio while lying in the bath. For a brief period while I studied for A Levels, the charts were all that mattered. I listened to *Parade of the Pops*, and followed Alan Freeman with his pop-pickers jingles on Sunday evenings. But then my tastes changed again, growing fiercer and more intense when I went to university.

My first encounter with the blues was in a darkened room, in a circle of friends. What they knew and approved was a whole new experience for me. I was stirred by the voices of John Lee Hooker, Buddy Guy and Muddy Waters, by their powers of resistance and that strange, choppy, raw blues feel that comes out of sadness and oppression. They were rough and cool and at times ecstatic, unlike anything I'd heard before, and I played my roommate's collection repeatedly.

From the blues I moved, inevitably, to Hendrix, absorbing myself in his wild, jagged rhythms and virtuoso guitar work. At times his instrument sounded like a jet breaking the sound barrier. He was noisy, dramatic and full of fired-up intensity, all of which suited my rebellious feelings. And to me his diminished fifths and clashing harmonies challenged the world I'd been living in.

With that idea in mind, I took *Are You Experienced?* home and played it to my parents. But my attempts to 'educate' them failed. After a long pause they simply commented that whatever it was 'sounded depressing' and nothing more was said.

Years later, I wrote a poem about listening to the radio in the bath and playing Hendrix to my parents:

### Encounter

1.

Fingering the dial of a small transistor
while he maps out the new on wall tile and plaster
he listens low-volume
as he stretches in the bath.

Pop charts in chorus, uh-huh-huhs,

the hey girl calls, yeah-yeah-yeah
and this week's climber would, if heard,
set off imperatives
with stops and starts and explanation sought,
then big-bodied sighs and *my house* grumbles
threatening from below.

Best kept low. Sky-dish-listening,
hoarse and whispering and out there to the stars.
Or fierce at a distance night-voiced, sweaty,
the singer steaming want *the latest,*
*the greatest* with passion beating up.
Now loud. Now louder.

2.

And then came Hendrix.
After rollups, substances and all-electric storms
at term-time parties he'd returned all innocence
to the hot-tongued, thick-pile silence
of vintage-motor placemats and roses behind glass.
No dead routine could hold him.
Now at last he'd be heard.

Persuaded, they sat back with coffee cups
and smiles, gazing towards the patterns
just above his head. "The blues," he'd warned them,
absorbed it seemed as actor or hero
in big-leap calculations of cliff drops between waves.

But at least, though doubtful, they'd pushed themselves
this far.

One world to another, he listened on a high.
Steel sounds, thunder, darkness, drums.
A long shot? Maybe. Or deep-breath gesture
to win them around by art.

Three tribal dances, then off.
Then nothing. Then stares.
Like that moment between acts
when doubt blocks applause,

or first time meeting on a far-distant shore
between proud-eyed painted warrior
and surprised explorer
both halted, empty-handed, wondering what to say.

It wasn't until I was past forty that I discovered, while learning music, that listening and performing are two very different experiences. My chosen instrument was a black upright Yamaha that I played late at night with the quiet pedal down. Although I put in hours, driven by the belief that I could achieve concert standard, I only reached grade five. My scales weren't smooth, I had to force myself through difficult passages and my sight reading was jittery. I also discovered that getting around the keyboard required rubber fingers and hands of steel. It was painful, unnatural and largely mechanical. So I learned the hard way, with tight forearms and an aching back, trying to please my teacher, who kept on stopping me and making me redo passages slowly and exactly to eliminate errors. It made me realise how much rote learning goes into any work of art.

Schopenhauer said that music is a universal language that speaks of the essence. He regarded music as the purest art because it was least representational. My experience was that it did indeed lift me, by removing the familiar and, in the words of Stravinsky,[2] 'digesting time'. Inside the music was a space more abstract than real, a standstill spot where for a moment I could be above myself. It didn't come easily — I'd forced myself to listen, wallowing in feeling and putting myself at the centre of it all. But what began as artificial became, through effort and practice, more natural. And in the end, the music I listened to became less a part of me and more a thing in itself: a lingua franca that takes us out of ourselves — what Schopenhauer called 'A copy of desire itself'... Or as Heine said: *When words leave off, music begins ...*

---

2 Often misquoted as W.H. Auden through misreading the preposition 'he' in Stravinsky: Chronicle of a Friendship, by Robert Craft (New York: Alfred A. Knopf, 1972), p. 6.

# THE ART OF GARDENS

According to the *Attention Restoration Theory*,[1] people can concentrate better after spending time in nature. A.R.T., developed by Rachel and Stephen Kaplan, divides attention into two types: 'Directed' and 'Effortless'.

Directed attention, typically office work, takes time and effort to achieve controlled focus and often involves putting a limit on emotion and movement. This kind of tight concentration comes at a price, so it's usually dependent on other knowledge and skills and can be easily broken by a single interruption, e.g. a telephone call. It's also fatiguing, causing people to become distracted, irritable, impatient and less effective in performing their tasks.

Effortless attention is where the mind is drawn in by the ever changing 'soft fascinations' to be found in nature, such as clouds moving across the sky, leaves rustling in a breeze or water bubbling over rocks in a stream. The results are restorative. The connected *Biophilia hypothesis* argues that people are instinctively enthusiastic about nature and that the positive psychological effect increases as the perceived biodiversity of the landscape increases.

So, after medical surgery, patients resting in rooms overlooking trees recovered better than those in rooms with only a view of a brick wall,[2] as did women recovering from breast cancer if they walked in a park, watched birds, or tended flowers.[3]

Similarly, researchers at Tokyo's Nippon Medical School have found that practising *shinrin-yoku*, or 'forest bathing' — a consciously reflective walk through a forest — increases the number of white cells in the human immune system.[4]

---

1 Kaplan, R. & Kaplan, S. (1989). The Experience of Nature: A Psychological Perspective. Cambridge University Press. ISBN 0-521-34139-6.
2 Ulrich, R. (1984).
3 Cimprich, B. (2007). Attention Restoration Theory: Empirical Work and Practical Applications.
4 Li, Qing (2010). Effect of forest bathing trips on human immune function. Environ Health Prev Med. 2010 Jan; 15(1): 9–17. Published online 2009 Mar 25.

The A.R.T. theory fits with my experience of visiting great gardens such as Hidcote or Sissinghurst. I've spent hours with my present wife, Sue, browsing their borders and green walks. We take our time, naming flowers and pointing out colour variation, or sitting looking out over water and rocks — and we're alert without effort, completely in the moment and holding hands. When we move on, it's at a slow pace on winding paths and steps through arches that take us out of ourselves and into what seems like imaginary time. So we might go back to the jungle when walking under Gunnera, associate monks with herbs, or picture Victorians with Heliotrope. And what we see we enjoy, like children in a secret garden. Of course, there are other tourists, too, taking pictures and look-ing at maps. It's a place for sitting, swatting flies and rubbing in sunblock. On rainy days it's an umbrella walk with the flowers bowed down and the pool spotting white. On those days, Sue and I stand by the wall, waiting for the rain to pass. When it does, we tour the borders, speaking occasion-ally, and maybe picking up petals from the ground. Soon it's hot again and the bees begin to circle. The sun brings out the butterflies — one lands on stone and folds up its wings. At a corner, Sue's close to a rosebud, taking in its scent. "Smell that," she says and I press my face up to the petals. The scent is faint: sweet lemon ice and coconut.

We walk on together, hearing a bird calling through leaves, and feeling the garden all around, filling up the air with fresh shoots and growth. It's a place of light and shade, of many shapes and moods, where our minds and bodies become part of everything — and softly, gently, the garden takes over

'Annihilating all that's made
To a green thought in a green shade ...'

Each garden is different. Some are laid out in rooms with screening hedges and connecting doorways, some are wooded with rocks and streams and rhododendron valleys, some are botanical, others are land-scaped, there are kitchen gardens and roof gardens and water gardens and terraces full of massed bulbs — all of them shaped and maintained, kept in check by a guiding hand, yet going their own way.

A few more types of garden:
♪   whispering places with eucalyptus and bamboo
♪   scented spots with peeling bark
♪   glassed-in winter gardens
♪   ferneries in caves and sunless quarries
♪   wired climbers on high city walls
♪   mythical gardens — Hesperides, Eden, Babylon, Lumbini, Ashok Vati-

ka and Xanadu
♪   Peace gardens, Zen gardens, permaculture gardens
♪   gardens of remembrance.

When we walk in a garden, Sue quickly loses herself in the sensual experience while I'm more divided. I'm by her side, sharing her feelings, but part of me keeps an eye on the route. I enjoy discovery and exploring new paths while for Sue every scene is new. She takes photos, posting them on Facebook, while I write poems about gardens and love. Here's one I wrote after a visit:

### Hidcote

We kiss. Paint squares hinge back.
The tulips are on-screen. There is blossom here too.
Falling from above the sun applies whitener.
Birds drift the path. The blossom sweats.
Powdered and stretched, they all say *ah*.

These blossoms are front row. Come dancing they say.
Oh yes, sing the birds. Hotspots develop.
Picking out partners, they advance upon the tulips.
Their mouths press red. Red, red-white.
Birds hop the sun. Confetti flurries thicken in the cups.

Another of our pastimes after a visit is the 'mental traveller game' where we talk through where we've been, step by step. It's a highlights tour, swopping plant names and comparing what we've seen, this time and the last. So we retell our stories with the aim, as Anaïs Nin said, 'to taste life twice, in the moment and in retrospect'. It brings us together, and imprints our memories with a shared view. And the story is about us, as lovers in a garden, and how *the moment in the rose garden / The moment in the arbour when the rain beat* can bring two people together. In the words of Sydney Eddison: 'Gardens are a form of autobiography'.

In the extract that follows from my novel *Blue*, I wanted to explore the idea that a garden is a reserved space where anything can happen, including the comic and the absurd. It's the story of Vanessa and Richard, the novel's protagonists, taking a garden trip with their friends Doug and Ruth. Being outdoors in a hidden space brings out their youthful ebullience ...

They visited Manor Gardens the next weekend. Doug drove and Vanessa directed, taking the scenic route, climbing through fields, crossing bare hills and descending sharply into leafless valleys. As they journeyed south, a grey-yellow sun appeared between clouds. When Doug grew tired Ruth took over, revving on straights and braking into corners. As she drove she swore, repeatedly. Beside her, Vanessa provided the directions. Her task was to calm things.

They turned west at a castle and ran past farms in an undulating district, cruising by fields and tree-topped outcrops to arrive at a final line of hills. Here they did a loop to descend beneath a scarp and enter the beginnings of a flat coastal plain.

"Soon be there," said Vanessa, aligning her map.

At a sign for Manor Gardens, Ruth slowed, swinging right into a winding country lane. The lane was narrow and muddy, with passing places.

"Well, it's a fun place to find," said Richard, gazing forward.

Close in to the hills, facing south, they entered a bowl-shaped valley laid out in terraces with steps down, dividing hedges, and early spring borders. "Cheers everyone, we're here," said Vanessa as they turned right through a gate.

"Mind your bums," called Ruth as they bumped across a cattle grid.

"Drrrrrrr," cried Richard.

They parked on grass and followed a track that dropped to a lodge where Richard paid, then passed in through an arch.

"It's south facing," said Vanessa leading along a pea gravel drive with banks both sides dotted with celandines and white and blue crocuses.

The path continued forward, past a birdbath lawn and up to a terrace beside a high-roofed house to reach a low-walled square. Here Ruth took Doug's arm. "Oh yes," she said gazing quietly at a large red camellia, "don't you just *feel* it."

For a while they walked the square, taking in the sunlight, the stone, the first shows on wood.

The square led to a narrow zigzag path with log steps and railings and a descent through trees. Here the grounds were wilder. They filed downhill past overspreading bushes, mostly just in bud. Vanessa led with an all-knowing air, shadowed by Ruth who kept asking questions; the two men followed, saying nothing.

At the bottom they came across a flat grassy spot and a dried-out pool. It was bare to the front and bushy around the edges. In the centre was a thick green awning with a swing bench beneath. "Rest spot," said Vanessa, rather grandly. They approached, exchanging glances.

"Come on, all aboard, room for everyone," cried Ruth, who was first to climb in. They packed the seat with Ruth and Doug in the middle, Richard at one end and Vanessa at the other. The view forward was panoramic.

For a while they talked gardens and childhood holidays until Ruth, losing interest, began pushing out. One leg to the floor, she was using her body as a counterweight. "It sags," she laughed, foot-rocking harder. The seat began to sway, creaking quietly and scraping at the sides. When she pushed again, using both feet, Vanessa joined in and the seat began to lurch.

"Careful," called Doug as the frame started to shudder.

Ruth lifted her legs, leaning with the movement, and the seat became a gondola. "Flying," she called and threw herself back, breaking into song.

"Hey!" shouted Doug, flushing.

Vanessa laughed. The seat was in motion, dipping and chopping like a rowboat. "Flying!" she echoed pushing at the frame, and the motion shifted sideways. She pushed again and the seat began to tack, corner to corner. It rose up, sidelong and back, describing a parabola, hitting on metal and jerking forward.

Doug called again.

At one end a wing nut flew off, clattering to the ground.

With a shout of "Flying!" the women kicked out together.

"This is silly," said Richard, gripping a bar.

"Very!" Ruth called, laughing.

"Bloody silly," he insisted, forcing the seat downwards. He continued, gripping heavily and swearing intermittently, until the seat came to rest.

Silence followed. In the bushes there were birds, rustling and calling. An elderly couple appeared, descending the hillside, holding the railing. Their voices sounded muffled, absorbed by wood.

Richard stood up and began searching for the nut. His expression was focused and purposeful. "Should be here," he told Vanessa, peering into grass and poking around the frame. Ruth joined in, ducking and stretching to peer beneath stones. Doug remained in place, feeling into corners and hand-checking where they'd sat.

In the course of the search Ruth moved up to Richard and offered an apology.

"No problem," he said.

They continued looking around. Apart from a spider-touch, with Ruth in shivers, and a few old coins found by Doug, nothing turned up.

"Best leave it," said Richard in the end. "Head for the hills. Vanish."

Ruth laughed, "You mean the Indian rope-trick?"

He grinned and licked his lips.

Vanessa glanced up the slope, "Shall we go?"

"One more look," called Doug, reaching sideways. As he moved, the seat began to drop. It shook and slipped, keeling sideways. "Wha—" he called, reaching into air. The bench went down, tipping still further. Doug cried out, one end collapsed and the canvas imploded like a badly-made tent. As it fell it rebounded, tipping him forward. He grabbed for the frame, missed, yelled and landed in a heap, rolling his eyes like a punch-drunk boxer.

"Oh my God!" squealed Ruth, hand to mouth.

"You all right?" asked Richard, crouching down.

Doug lay hunched, back to the questioner, shivering.

"Is he injured?"

Richard peered closer, frowning, "Not sure. You OK?"

Doug continued shaking.

"Are you all right?"

No reply.

"Doug—"

Ruth pushed forward. She peered at him, craning to one side, seeking a reply. "Hey there?" Almost as she spoke, Doug turned suddenly, baring his teeth and levering up. For a second he appeared hurt. Then, with a gasp, he stood pointing to the seat, doubling forward. "What a— What a—" he whooped, spluttering and shaking and dancing about. Arms out, he was windmilling both ways, as if he'd been stung.

Ruth stepped back, "You're all right then?"

Doug turned to face her, struggling for air. Before he could reply the others joined in, giggling and snorting. Even Ruth, after expressing surprise, was drawn into laughter.

They continued, high-stepping about and eyeballing each other. They'd entered, for a moment, a kind of charmed circle.

It was Vanessa who moved to the path, recalling them to purpose. "Uphill?" she asked, pointing. Her face was flushed, her body set forward.

When Doug began another dance she pointed harder. "Ladies and gentlemen," she insisted, "calmly please. We need to go."

Richard responded first. "Come on you lot," he said, looking upwards.

"Now," said Vanessa.

"At the double," said Ruth, gripping Doug's arm, who repeated the phrase as a question. When Ruth nodded he squared his shoulders and led off smartly, climbing through the trees.

The path back was steep and they moved in a line, throwing out comments and laughing wildly. At each turn in the path they grabbed the railing and tackled the reverse slope. As they neared the top Ruth stretched up, one-finger-shushing, cautioning them to silence. Suddenly they were children with a secret between them.

On the upper level they looked about. The air was still, the paths were clear and the flower heads were motionless. They walked and explored, circling around borders and passing through a wall. In this part of the gardens they were alone.

After forking right past rose beds they returned to the house, entering a conservatory through a half-glassed door. Inside, the air felt thick. A fine layer of mist had collected on the windows and the pipes. A tap in the corner was dripping onto tiles.

"Feel this. It's like stepping into a sauna," said Doug, squaring his shoulders.

An attendant stood close by. She was half-concealed behind a large glazed pot containing a butterfly palm. Beyond her was a glass and metal gallery with climbers on one side and a café at the end.

After agreeing they were hot, they asked the attendant about serving drinks and walked the full length to pull up chairs around a patterned metal table. Richard took orders and set off to collect. During his absence the others gazed about. The corner they had occupied was tall and bare and painted white. Green around the edges, it was damp and echoed like a warehouse.

They were linked now by the occasional word: a reference, a tag phrase, a hand-rocking gesture and a slowly spreading grin. After bringing the coffees, Richard made an effort to switch to plant talk, but when Ruth mentioned flying and Vanessa began to splutter, the laughter took over, coming in waves. Small waves at first, then overlapping, ending in hand-gripping snorts as they rose and straightened and gazed out to the terrace, spluttering.

"Silly," said Richard, keeping it low.

"Bloody silly," whispered Ruth.

"Bloody, bloody silly."

"Silly, silly, silly."

"Bloody, bloody, bloody—"

They continued pacing, repeating in chorus. Behind them Vanessa and Doug had dropped out. They were in the audience, playing statues.

Seeing the attendant advancing from the doorway, Ruth pulled back. "I think," she said, steadying herself, "we may need to go."

Richard laughed, "And when you gotta—"

"Shhh," warned Vanessa, following Ruth's gaze.

"Careful," added Doug.

The attendant stepped around and back, staring at a point just to one side. She was tall and severe, wearing tweeds and a hat. Her movements were bird-like and edgy. When she'd finished her beat, returning to the doorway, Richard broke the silence. "Right," he said, "we'd best leave."

Ruth smiled thinly, "Pretend we weren't here?"

"Whatever it takes."

He began to walk and the other three joined him, moving back along the gallery. They advanced without looking left or right, ducking out through the garden door.

As they emerged a bell rang and a voice called out, echoing slightly. "I think it's closing," said Vanessa, looking up at the sky and distancing slightly. Beside her Richard drew one hand across his brow. Ruth and Doug brought up the rear, arms linked together.

They advanced along the terrace in silence. The sun was low, striking their faces and the air was still. In the square to one side the shadows were lengthening; on the other side, the walls of the house were bathed in brightness. In front were the steps down to the path beside the lawn.

The bell rang once, twice, and the voice called again.

"Time," said Ruth.

They descended the steps and crunched across gravel. When they reached the main drive the light had weakened. A drift of clouds had thinned the sunlight and a breeze was moving gently, shifting over grass. The bell rang again, followed by the voice — a single syllable. On the banks both sides the crocuses were closing.

As they passed out through the lodge Richard took Vanessa by the hand. "The voice in the garden," he said quietly, glancing around.

Nodding she turned and together, saying nothing, they walked back to the car.

This passage was loosely based on a visit Sue and I paid to Kiftsgate Court Gardens in the Cotswolds. When we were there, the upper level was full of huge pink and red peonies. The timing of the passage, in early spring, led naturally to celandines and crocuses and, since they needed a setting, I used the actual pea gravel driveway — though it doesn't have flowerbeds. The wooded drop with its panoptic views exists, but it doesn't face south, the real pool isn't dry and the conservatory they climb back up to was grafted on from another stately home. The mood at the end was suggested, of course, by the story of the expulsion from the Garden of Eden.

So it's a garden of the mind, arranged around the season, that sets out to put the characters through their paces. As a foursome, taken out of their usual surroundings, they become childlike and reckless: they overstep the mark and have to leave the garden, returning to adulthood. The incident is a cameo version of how Richard and Vanessa choose risk and conflict to reawaken their failing marriage, coming close to the edge before accepting their limits.

So the book's a walk in the gallery of the mind where everything's alive and significant and charged with meaning. And writing a novel is like planting a garden that soon runs wild. Nothing is fixed: times and places run together, characters take on a life of their own, while at any moment a new phrase can pop up and the story changes. Books are like the weather, and each carefully-chosen element only holds up in relation to the whole. As Baudelaire said: 'A book is a garden, an orchard, a storehouse, a party, a company by the way, a counsellor, a multitude of counsellors'. Or, in the words of Cicero: 'If you have a garden and a library, you have everything you need'.

*The best characters are complex — what you see depends on how you look at them.*

*Writing is a journey controlled by character and feel. Plot emerges naturally, riskily from style and vocabulary.*

*What I tell myself as an author: work at language, edit, rewrite, find the perfect phrase, then rewrite again; it has a voice of its own.*

# 2nd MOVEMENT

## LIVING WITH IMAGINATION

### What readers said about:
*Robin Gregory Interviews Leslie Tate*
and
*Talking to My Teenage Self*

There's something both very difficult and very special in writing about the people closest to you. I found Leslie Tate's description of his mother and father, of their lives and their character traits, to be both honest and revealing. I was touched by the way he talked about their frailties and deficiencies as well as about his fond memories of them. It chimed with my feelings about my own parents as a child and made me think about those times, bringing them back to me vividly as they once were in a Proustian rush.
— *Chris Hill, Author of Song of the Sea God and The Pick-up Artist.*

*Living With Imagination* is an analysis of a developing psyche in post war UK: the struggles of a baby boomer to make sense of his upbringing in a strict nuclear family — and at the same time realising something of the struggles his father and mother endured through the Thirties and Forties. It's never an easy thing to write about yourself, make it interesting, witty, objective and relevant, but Leslie Tate pulls it off with aplomb, irony and brilliant touches of pathos, making it a very engaging read. What also comes out of this fascinating piece is how you cannot separate your own personal growth from your journey as a writer: '... the best writing comes out of what's most difficult. The task is to look at it unflinchingly and write it.' A great read.
— *Neil Beardmore, Dramatist, Novelist, Poet, Artist and Musician.*

This is powerful and exposing prose which draws character in nuanced detail, creating an explanation of time and place as well as the people it describes. We are all the sum of our past (to misquote!) and this writing invites us to consider whether creativity stems from an ability to recognise that sum's quali-

ties.
— *Clare Sayers, Reader, Linguist and Specialist Teaching Assistant.*

An intriguing insight into the development of a writer, how the experiences, conflicts, pressures and differences shape not only the person but the creative process. And how the creative process in turn can bring resolution and peace.
— *Izzy Robertson, Author and Complementary Therapist.*

I thought the dialogue with self was a brilliant concept and very thought-provoking. It read just like a real-time conversation that I was eaves-dropping in on. The ending was perfect.
— *Virginia Moodie, retired Social Worker.*

In three enticing and enhancing ways — an interview, a poem and a conversation piece — Leslie Tate brings us intimately into the world of his childhood and adolescence.
— *Hazel Ward, retired Adult Education Tutor and Manager.*

# ROBIN GREGORY'S AUTHOR PROFILE OF LESLIE TATE

*http://madmysticaljourney.com/blog.html*

**Robin**: Where were you born and raised? Can you tell us a little about your family?

**Leslie**: I was born and brought up in suburban North London as an only child. My dad was a tall, dark-haired tax inspector who, as he got older, wore baggy pants and jumpers at home, chain smoked, and became increasingly dissatisfied with his job. He was born in rural Northumberland and had studied hard to win a scholarship place at Middlesborough High School, so he felt passed over when young men who had been to Oxbridge — an opportunity he was denied because of fighting in the Second World War — were promoted above him. He was complex. So he could be slick with cuff links and ties, he could be funny making Goon-like noises, he was clever with figures, but mostly he was deeply serious — obsessively reading fact and fiction about the war. During my little-boy-admirer period (which went on longer than most: I was slow to mature) I read *The Cruel Sea* by Nicolas Monsarrat and *HMS Ulysses* by Alistair MacLean, thinking they were the greatest novels ever written. He once told me an odd story, saying that he'd chanced upon the first four notes of Beethoven's Fifth Symphony on the piano before hearing the original. By then I'd read Freud and, to my shame, I rubbished his claim, overlooking its true meaning. Behind the mask of a doggedly dependable family man he had wildly romantic dreams of conducting his own symphonies, and his greatest frustration was not having time to do it. Sadly, much of his creative drive got lost in the detail. So he'd duplicate the patterns from marquetry kits, paint by numbers or measure out a garden path within fractions of an inch, like the surveyor he'd once been in the war. Though oddly, an anarchist streak in him resulted in bodged DIY and Heath Robinson repairs to fixtures and furniture, and temporary fixes to household machines that soon broke down. He was diligently practical, over-careful, exacting of himself, gruffly willing, and deeply disappointed.

My mum's still alive. She's a short, light-haired, round-faced woman who is quick on the uptake and very strong willed. Brought up in a N.E. England musical family, with her father conducting the local seaside choir and her mother playing piano and organ, she was more interested in fashion and dancing. She met my dad when his parents moved in next door and they went out biking, often riding as far as the Lake District. Even today she enjoys the idea of adventure and 'being an individual' while holding onto a traditional set of values. It's this split between ideal and performance that makes her impatient with herself and others, wanting things done yesterday. She's a busy woman, a skilled knitter and a modernist gardener with an interest in politics and travel, who hates 'wasting time' and can push herself too hard sometimes, straining her 90 year-old body in an effort to 'get things done'. As a gardener she battles with her plants, 'chopping' them and subjecting them to her will. She has been known to compare raising children to breaking horses, although she's also critical of the Fifties idea of 'not praising children because it makes them conceited'. For her, the big problem in bringing me up was that the maternity hospital separated us for the first two weeks and she only saw me at feeding times. When we got home she'd been drilled to feed every four hours, her milk flow was poor and I screamed for more. We both became pale, thin and exhausted. Now, when she talks about my upbringing she looks at me challengingly and calls me a 'difficult child'. I make a point of contradicting her, partly because I need to rediscover the child I really was, but also because I think she's actually talking about my later, youthful rebellion.

I believe my childhood was insecure, not just because of the experience in hospital but also because both my parents were moody. Although they tried hard to be 'fair' and 'reasonable' it came across to me as harshly reactive. So I see myself trying to be helpful, setting out tablemats and drawing curtains, but then next day it's time to change the sheets and I'm upstairs bouncing on the bed until, quite suddenly, I'm smacked by my mother for getting in the way. I think I'd been 'told', maybe I ignored her, but I wasn't quick-witted. The shift between good boy and bad boy, from nice to nasty, didn't make sense. All I knew was there was a darkness in the house, an unrealised feeling of struggle and effort and my parents were, at times, tired of life and unpredictable.

As I grew older I blamed them for everything. In my mind they'd kept me cooped up and under continuous scrutiny, wanting to know when I went out, where I was going, for how long, and when I'd be back. I objected to their exact routines and by-the-clock meals, I felt they were running me down with remarks like 'You're not like that' and I regarded their obsessive, niggling concerns for my health as over-controlling. So I took issue with their worldview, challenging their opinions and arguing vehemently with my dad at supper time, calling him a 'warmonger'. In short, I thought I knew better — which translated in Sixties speak to *I want my freedom.*

**Robin:** How did you start writing? Did anyone specifically encourage you?

**Leslie:** From an early age I was 'writing my life' as a running commentary in my head. Part of this was a *Boy's Own* narrative of war and heroism and Biggles-like adventures. Another part was solitary play where I drew maps in sand and dramatised meetings with neighbours, teachers and famous people. The third part was more clandestine — and this was the beginning of my real writing — where I fantasized about switching gender to make an appearance in *Alice in Wonderland*, then later read and recited Romantic poems. But my own efforts weren't in the same league. I was in my Shelley period, writing turgid 'atmospheric' poems about magical landscapes weighed down with adjectives and archaic language. I took this all very seriously, sitting down in the dining room a few times to recite *Ode to the West Wind* into a tape recorder. My version was grandly theatrical as I lifted my voice to imitate a storm — gushing and hollering and straining for effect — but my mum and dad took no notice, probably thinking that if they ignored me I'd soon lose interest.

Years later, I wrote a poem about my hyped-up intensity and my dad's parallel, but much more serious, obsession with Orwell and Koestler and totalitarianism. The irony of the poem is that both generations are self-dramatising, the boy parades his fragility as a kind of 'world sucks' accusation, the parents are dug into defensive routines and Thirties nightmares.

### Rhetorics

'O! lift me as a wave, a leaf, a cloud!
I fall upon the thorns of life! I bleed!'
From *Ode to the West Wind*, Shelley

The front room is the boy's. He's in there with Shelley
reading to a tape. Outside it is hot.
From low to high, shifting, impatient,
the big words gush, straining towards love.

Inhaling to a glow in the shaded back garden
his father considers final solutions to the late summer

blackfly and leaf curl on the peach.
His mother used soapsuds. The next doors blew smoke.

A bird calls quickly, chattering through the hedge.
A wasp digs brickwork. The grandfather chimes.
They, too, had their rhetorics from tealeaves on roses
to card tricks and braces, speeches at Christmas,
songbooks, Polos and sweeteners in milk.
For them it was the way.

See now what followed, as newsreels pass
of torchlight faces, crowd-surge, ecstatics
and the smooth-tongued, spot-lit prosecutor
pausing before climax for effect.

Darkness at Noon. The Ministry of Truth.
Or bad dramatics.

And now, behind the door, his thee-and-thouing, high-voiced son,
reading so it hurts. From surprised reverential,
to windblown in snatches, then full-force
long-distance, shouting on the phone,
to feather-breath on glass.

To a single, dissolute finger-curl of smoke
trailing to a thread, or lifelong ache floated into air,
from tiptoe arching youth who holds himself private
while working into rhetoric
for fear of what's to come.

But most of my youthful poems were 'lived' not written down. I wandered
neglected farm tracks feeling elevated and close to the spirit world while
recording every detail on a tape loop in my head. The hush was all around
and my exclusion was a mark, a sign of my election, putting me beyond
the reach of parental supervision and bullies at school. I walked for miles,
consciously cultivating my closeness to nature, quoting Wordsworth and
imagining myself as a pilgrim journeying the wilderness while thinking of
higher things.

I did things I shouldn't. There were other forces in the bushes, spirit
watchers who tempted me from the path. So, looking around quickly, I'd
duck behind a bunker or take cover in woods where I'd hide my clothes

and strut back and forth, enjoying my nakedness. My hand did the rest. Afterwards I'd dodge back to my hideout to emerge fully dressed, sweating, and fearful of discovery. When I reached home I put it all behind me and resumed my life, but I wasn't myself. I believed that what I'd done had marked me out. At the time I was reading *Paradise Lost*, so I went about with an abandoned feeling, a proudly defiant sense of knowing what others didn't; I'd gone wrong, I didn't like myself, and sooner or later I — or the world — would pay for it.

Perhaps it was this split between the dignified truths of books and the messiness of life that stopped me writing. I wanted my words on the page to come quickly, from above, showing life as it should be, but the poems I wrote seemed flat and laboured. Behind my predictable turns of phrase there was a whole range of secret obsessions I believed couldn't be touched — not only my onanism but also my narcissistic relationship to the mirror and, crucially, my hidden cross-dressing. Those acts weighed me down; they made me untouchable. My poetic persona was a defensive mechanism, a don't-look-now plea for forgiveness, but only skin deep. I'd never be able to write honestly about my own disgusting habits. In any case, how could I possibly be a writer, given the unpleasant reality of my secret life?

The other blocks were social. My parents came from a 'no nonsense' background and thought music was important but distrusted poetry, while the rule at school was to stick to the syllabus and treat with suspicion anything fancy or contrived. I remember writing a fantasy about falling off a cliff, packing it with adjectives and figures of speech, and the collective amusement — led by the teacher — when I read it out in class.

**Robin**: So how did you get from there to being published?

**Leslie**: I realised later in life that being a writer is no more than a persuasion: a label you give yourself, a title or calling that goes beyond sales figures or being in print. To write originally you have to go out on a limb and ditch all your preconceptions. My desire to write was kept alive by reading T.S. Eliot as well as novelists like D.H. Lawrence and Dostoyevsky. It stayed with me at university, although still out of reach, kept at a distance by my habit of putting off, trying out new writers, reading psychology, philosophy, sociology, politics, and 'banking' experience for when I'd finally put pen to paper. It was still there, provisionally, when I became a teacher and wrote occasional poetry. It survived, as Auden says:

In the valley of its making where executives
Would never want to tamper, flows on south

From ranches of isolation and the busy griefs,
Raw towns that we believe and die in; it survives,
A way of happening, a mouth.

— until I met my present wife, Sue Hampton, and began writing professionally — every day, as a routine, as I am now, filling up the space with imaginary characters and words as music plucked out of the air, like Caliban hearing Ariel.

**Robin**: How is *Purple* important to you? Has writing it helped you explore and/or heal unresolved issues from the past?

**Leslie**: Like my parents, I wouldn't be beaten. Every knock to my confidence from childhood onwards simply made me more determined. Of course rejection hurts but, like all pain, it's there for a purpose. It proves you're alive and may kick-start action. The challenge, I knew, was to listen, go with it, and write about the conflicts and the hidden absurdities that people don't own up to.

It took four days to fashion the first sentence and many years before it reached the present form — which I still regard as unfinished. I've added two more books, *Blue* and *Violet* and a network of family relationships based on the idea that 'things get passed down'.

Writing it came out of that hole in my childhood: all those strange, shameful feelings and mental acrobatics designed to conceal what I'd been up to. I was saved by the imagination, by the intake of breath I always feel when a book does something daring, and the power of words to reshape experience. Finally I'd understood that the best writing comes out of what's most difficult. The task is to look at it unflinchingly and write it.

**Robin**: What are one or two things you would most like to tell aspiring writers?

**Leslie**: Seek out your most embarrassing moments and get to know them as your friends and allies. As you rework them they will guide your way.

Examine your own writing to find your true voice. Once you've found it, take that as your starting point and delete all the rest.

# TALKING TO MY TEENAGE SELF

**Me, Adult:** Have you ever really thought about what your parents did for you? Life wasn't easy for them. They were worried about you.

**Me, Teen:** What's there to worry about?

**Adult:** It shows they cared.

**Teen:** About themselves?

**Adult:** Hold on. Your dad thought the world of you.

**Teen:** Yeah, as long as I fitted into *his* world. Did you know he wanted me to be a tax inspector like him?

**Adult:** He wanted you to do well, that's all. It's natural to a parent. Protect and survive. He could see what you were doing to yourself.

**Teen:** I hope not. That sounds horrible.

**Adult:** I mean, he knew what was wrong.

**Teen:** He did? Then why didn't *he* do something about it?

**Adult:** He saw how withdrawn you were.

**Teen:** Of course, it takes one to know one.

**Adult:** That's not really—

**Teen:** You know what withdrawn is? It's when you keep spouting your opinions but you're deaf to anything coming back the other way. So, let's be honest and talk about what really happened — we fought. I was his rival, his sparring partner — father v son, the big match, slugging it out every supper time. I used to hate it. We'd both go on claiming this and that, saying anything, it didn't really matter, as long as we got the last word. My dad reckoned he knew *everything*.

**Adult:** He taught you chess. Without him driving you to competitions you'd never have become British Under 21s Champion.

**Teen:** Yeah, but chess was a safe option. I gave it up later.

**Adult:** What do you mean, 'safe option'?

**Teen:** It was what was allowed. I wanted to play music but he said our piano was too old and out of tune. So I settled on

|          |                                                                 |
|----------|-----------------------------------------------------------------|
|          | second best.                                                    |
| **Adult:** | Dad did try to teach you sport.                               |
| **Teen:** | His sport. Cricket.                                             |
| **Adult:** | And he took you to concerts.                                   |
| **Teen:** | You should have heard him on Debussy.                          |
| **Adult:** | You gardened together.                                         |
| **Teen:** | It's like the other stuff. I wanted to please.                 |
| **Adult:** | And he helped you with Maths.                                  |

**Teen:** Let me tell you about that. I was supposed to listen and be grateful. And I did and I was, in a way. But nothing he said made any sense. He thought it was all obvious so he just *told* me, and kept on repeating when I didn't get it. It's like when people shout at someone who's deaf. It just makes things worse. I don't think he'd any idea why numbers are difficult for some people. He left me feeling I was stupid.

**Adult:** But you were lucky, compared with them. Your parents gave you a good education, a decent home and money in your pocket. You didn't want for much.

**Teen:** Oh, *that* one. 'Just be thankful lad, you had it easy' — that's what they said, on and on. You had to be grateful for a bed to sleep in, a roof over your head and shoes on your feet — otherwise they'd take them away. They used to threaten me with being kicked out, you know. Only a few times, to be honest, but I was in a panic when I thought about it. In my mind I heard them saying *and what would you do then?* I didn't believe I could stand on my own feet — and that came from somewhere ...

**Adult:** So you blame them?

**Teen:** Yeah I do, mainly. The story was that I was completely impractical. Of course I had my reply ready to throw at them, which was they'd kept me in cotton wool, so what did they expect? I know, I know, people in glass houses shouldn't throw stones. But the truth was I'd no idea where to begin — all those adult things like jobs and money and getting a house — well, going out in the world was pretty scary.

**Adult:** A lot of young people feel that way. Starting out is hard.

**Teen:** They could've made it easier. They were antisocial, you know. The world out there was big and bad and nasty. They didn't really have any friends. Later on, when we

|          |                                                                 |
| -------- | --------------------------------------------------------------- |
|          | moved to Northumberland, they cut themselves off.               |
| **Adult:** | Why was that, do you think?                                   |
| **Teen:** | I dunno. There was something wrong. They drew up the drawbridge and that was it. They were afraid of something bad happening, that's all I can say. |
| **Adult:** | Both of them?                                                 |
| **Teen:** | Pretty well. My mum went along with it. I know she was a bit of a risk-taker when she was young, so something changed. Maybe it was all the talk about the war — whatever it was, she started to act like we were under siege. |
| **Adult:** | Do you remember that chess quote, 'The threat is stronger than its execution'? |
| **Teen:** | Of course.                                                   |
| **Adult:** | I think it applies.                                          |
| **Teen:** | You mean it was a tactic?                                     |
| **Adult:** | I'm talking about the psychology. How it worked on them.     |
| **Teen:** | Ah, I get it. You mean when people are scared of their own shadow. I remember that feeling. Like the story where a boy barricades himself into his bedroom, to keep something weird outside. In the middle of the night he wakes up, hearing a noise. He reaches for the matches and the box is placed in his hand. Then a voice whispers close to his ear, "That's good. Now we're alone and no one can get in." |
| **Adult:** | Now that's what I call a cautionary tale.                    |
| **Teen:** | Yeah, I reckon they spooked themselves out. They seemed to think the world was against them, as if they were living in enemy territory. |
| **Adult:** | What you might call fear of fear.                            |
| **Teen:** | *It's behind you*, eh?                                        |
| **Adult:** | Yes. And that's the hardest thing to come to terms with. And not just when you're young. I'm still afraid of the dark. I sleep with the landing light on, and if I get up for a pee I edge along the wall, ready to do battle. |
| **Teen:** | Really? You do? Why's that, d'you think?                     |
| **Adult:** | Oh, it's as you said — the house was full of bottled-up feelings. All the unspoken stuff. As a child, you live in the adults' shadow ... You were afraid of ghosts? |
| **Teen:** | And how. I remember the fear of being watched from behind. Everywhere I went there were eyes drilling in, |

|              | but when I spun round there was nothing there. Kind of creepy. |
| Adult:       | Yes, you wonder if you made it up, or it was something about you. But of course it was real, and the fact that it sticks years later, shows just how real. The whole place felt like the scene of a crime. |
| Teen:        | A crime? What kind of crime? |
| Adult:       | An inside job, maybe ... I remember there were always suspicions. To their way of thinking, people were not to be trusted. I'd go as far as to say other people to them were *things*. Either that or they blanked the lot, reducing it to a formula — living, I mean — into a kind of lock-down. You had to toe the line, and be practical, practical, practical. What's in it for me, that kind of thing. They measured everything by what you did and what you got for it. |
| Teen:        | I think you're being a bit harsh. |
| Adult:       | Didn't you feel it that way? |
| Teen:        | Well, not like you just said. Not so one-sided. |
| Adult:       | So you think I'm exaggerating? |
| Teen:        | Not exactly. But you have to see it from their side as well. It wasn't easy. |
| Adult:       | You mean they weren't to blame? |
| Teen:        | Listen, they were brought up to a different world. I've looked at the pictures. Men had to fight and women weren't taken seriously. To get to where they did was a big effort and it took it out of them. They had to get on with it. |
| Adult:       | You know, sometimes you make me laugh. |
| Teen:        | How come? |
| Adult:       | I'd have thought it was obvious. |
| Teen:        | Obvious? How? |
| Adult:       | Well, don't take this wrong, but you're sounding like *them*. |
| Teen:        | If I am, so what? Isn't that bound to be so? |
| Adult:       | Not necessarily. You can't use upbringing as your excuse. You have to be aware. Otherwise you end up repeating ... |
| Teen:        | The same mistakes? Come off it. Give me one thing you'd have done different if you were them. |
| Adult:       | You want me to tell you? |
| Teen:        | Go ahead. |

| | |
|---|---|
| **Adult:** | OK, moving house. You know what it was like. Always the outsider, starting a new school and getting picked on. I was a loner enough already, but that really did it. |
| **Teen:** | Was there a choice? They moved his work, he had to go. Simple as that. |
| **Adult:** | Mum didn't like it either. She really struggled. |
| **Teen:** | You haven't answered my question. What else could they do? |
| **Adult:** | My point is that it was a mess. Yours seems to be that it was a mess for everyone. |
| **Teen:** | Don't tell me what I said. |
| **Adult:** | So we all got screwed up. But that's OK. |
| **Teen:** | Have it your way then. The whole thing was a disaster and − hey look! − I'm a wreck. You know that song in West Side Story, 'We're disturbed, we're disturbed, we're psychologically disturbed ...' |
| **Adult:** | I didn't mean ... |
| **Teen:** | You didn't? I say you did. It gives you pleasure to be messed up. It's a badge of honour. Oh, poor me, you say. It's all about you and your feelings. As long as you can point at Mum and Dad and make out you're not to blame then that'll do ... |
| **Adult:** | You don't have to be like that. |
| **Teen:** | Just saying what I think. |
| **Adult:** | But the way you put things ... |
| **Teen:** | You're not happy? |
| **Adult:** | I don't think it's true. |
| **Teen:** | I admit it's an opinion. Mine. But I didn't want to upset you. Sorry. |
| **Adult:** | All right, let's suppose we each take a step back. Now, I realise I may have said unhelpful things. |
| **Teen:** | You did? What you thinking of? |
| **Adult:** | What I said at the start. |
| **Teen:** | Ah, that. Well, my memory's very bad, so you're going to have to help me ... |
| **Adult:** | You mean a repeat? |
| **Teen:** | Yes. |
| **Adult:** | You kidding? |
| **Teen:** | Yes, in a way. But again − please. |
| **Adult:** | Well ... Have you ever thought ... No, have *we* ever thought ... Hang on, this doesn't sound right ... |

| | |
|---|---|
| **Teen:** | I'll finish. Have we ever really thought what our parents did for us? |
| **Adult:** | Really thought? |
| **Teen:** | Or really, really thought? |
| **Adult:** | That's it. |
| **Teen:** | That's right. |
| **Adult:** | Yes. |
| **Teen:** | Yes. |
| **Adult:** | Well, we have now ... |

*When I write my characters are the story. I listen to the words to find out what's next. Things develop. People change. That way it stays fresh.*

*What makes a good novel? It makes you think and feel and dream and observe and reflect and understand your place in the world.*

*Because the action of a modern novel goes on in the minds of the characters, one small incident can open up a world of possibilities.*

# 3rd MOVEMENT

## *CHILDHOOD*

**What readers said about:**

*The Past is Another Country*    *It's the Journey that Counts*
*The Way of Imagination*    *My Secret Life*
*For the Losers*    and    *The Dark Side*

In *Heaven's Rage* boyhood is a fragile teacup carried scene to scene, as if youth were bone china captured in free-fall. 'Everything's in motion,' Leslie Tate says. How frightening and lonely it is for a child to have nothing to cling to. A beautifully stark and poetic portrait of boyhood.
— *Robin Gregory, Author of the Improbable Adventures of Moojie Littleman.*

So often these trips down memory lane are a vehicle for self-indulgent internalized angst. This, however, was different. Rather than mawkish, it was poignant, rather than angry, it was reflective. It was a moving and honest account of a challenging journey through early youth and adolescence. Particularly notable for me was the contrast of past and present and Leslie Tate's cool control of language and emotion as he examined the 'fresh perspective' that distance and maturity had lent him. This was a fascinating read, balanced by dark and light and full of sincerity and charm.
— *Melanie Whipman, Author, Editor and Lecturer at Chichester University.*

There is vulnerability here and quiet strength. There is light, shade and a palpable darkness. All of it enthralls. The child's resilience, the combination of a vivid imagination and felt experience, confirming childhood as both a journey and a battleground.
— *Katie Willis, finalist in Spread The Word and Bristol Short Story Competitions.*

Anyone who's ever felt like an outsider looking into the goldfish bowl of life will be able to relate to Leslie Tate's imaginative autobiography, *Heaven's Rage*. In brave, soul-baring prose and poetry, he reveals how creativity — his 'magic thinking' — saved him from anxiety, low self-esteem and rejection. Leslie Tate's childhood habit of 'slotting into gaps where people wouldn't see [him]' left him

isolated but gave rise to a much-needed sense of security and freedom, enabling him to create, write about and explore his identity.
— *Liz Lockhart, Freelance Writer and Secretary of Grantham Writers.*

A beautiful and heartfelt journey of re-discovery. The narrative paints a picture of a lonely boy, living in solitude, with only his imagination for company. It's sometimes a painful read and a reminder of what life was like once the rose tinted glasses of memory are removed. Very powerful.
— *John Marsh, retired Civil Servant.*

Leslie Tate's account of his childhood surprises and discoveries brought back powerful memories of my own childhood as a deaf person. Growing up without hearing, you are left to make sense of the world as best you can. Sitting in a family get-together watching everyone chatting without having a clue what is going on. Not understanding what teachers were saying, and having to follow children with better hearing in the hope that I'd be going the right way and find out what was happening. Being excluded by the other children in my street from their games: they discovered that if they stood together chatting, I would get bored and wander off. As soon as I did, they started playing again. If I came back and tried to join in, they instantly got into their chatting group once more. It didn't take long for me to get the message there.

Even in mid-life, I still have a huge emotional reaction to being told off for doing things that I didn't know had been declared to be wrong. I intensely dislike the sort of scenario where you start off doing something new and are welcomed at first only to discover all the caveats and invisible rules as you go along.

I remember finding faces and animals in the lino on the bathroom floor when I was very small, and patterns in the clouds. The human brain is powerfully programmed to look for patterns in everything. We often remember the way people made us feel, rather than what actually happened.
— *Jill Hipson, BSL Teacher, BA Hons in English Literature.*

In the words of Aunt Lovey, in Lori Lansens's novel *The Girls* — 'Read and if you have a writer's voice, one day it will shout out "I can do that too!"' There is absolutely no doubt that Leslie Tate has a writer's voice and in *Heaven's Rage* he is showing us that he can, nay he must do that too.
— *Jackie Healy, Billet Lane Book Group.*

There is something for everyone to recognize and enjoy in this fascinating journey into the writer's childhood, capturing memories and seeking the roots of author-hood.
— *Yan Christensen, Berkhamsted.*

# THE PAST IS ANOTHER COUNTRY

*I felt the solidity of my adult life compared to the transparency of childhood. It was as if I'd glimpsed myself as another person in another time and place.*

Have you ever taken the nostalgia trip to where you used to live? Maybe to your old house, a school, a street or a childhood play space? Even if you haven't, you've probably thought about it. So what's it like? And what does it tell us, if anything, about ourselves? I imagined it would bring back memories and plug me in more directly to childhood. I also hoped it would tell me more about myself and start me off writing. But the experience wasn't quite what I'd expected.

My return to my first home in North London made me realise how much I had changed. Suddenly the house, which had seemed like a castle, was an average semi-D with a short front garden and a narrow side alley. Instead of looking up at the concrete front steps I faced it on the level. It was measured, suburban and unremarkable. My memories contained scenes of adventure climbing fences and imaginary escapes over roofs and chimney pots. Certainly, being there was emotional in a quiet way, but there wasn't the drama and magic I'd remembered. I was surprised that I'd lived in this ordinary place and found it so grand and exciting. I felt the solidity of my adult life compared to the transparency of childhood. It was as if I'd glimpsed myself as another person in another time and place.

While I was there I retraced the walk I took to school. The route was marked by cinema-like images of the overgrown wasteland with its hidden stalkers, the clinic where the nurse counted slowly with a needle in my arm and the back alley detours I took to avoid being followed. Painful memories which I can see as I write. Of course the route looked different but the new-build and the fences couldn't change the memories. The past remains inside us, in tight fists of feeling. It's a picture I find myself painting when, like now, I select from all those memories and take a point of view. What we choose to remember, and how we shape it, is who we are.

My next trip was to my old school in Northumberland. Again it was the painful memories that stood out: the cross-country runs with snow on the ground, the bullying, the boredom, the note-taking and tests. The school was the same — grey slate and blackened stone with muddy playing fields — but what it brought to mind was how much I'd wanted out. Behind the ordinary façade I could still feel the kick in the shins, the punch on the neck and the rubber-tube beating by my Maths teacher. The trip didn't change things because those memories are fixed inside, like blown-up photos taken at the scene of a crime. But instead of being the victim, I was the inspector checking through the evidence, able to see myself at a distance.

The last trip was to the seaside town where my grandparents lived. The memories here were of watching ten-foot waves breaking on concrete and all-day games playing on the beach. The adult eye saw an empty town with boarded-up amusements and abandoned buildings. But standing on the front I felt again that ridiculous, straining desire to escape. It's what's called the oceanic feeling. In trying to be a poet I trained myself to look at the clouds, reciting Shelley and working on my sense of aloneness. Perhaps I'd understood that spiritual elevation, like anything else, can be increased through training. But being there again made me think that my boyhood afflatus wasn't so silly after all. Without it I couldn't have that feeling of oneness with nature or know that what we call the 'poetic' may begin from being forced. The boy I'd connected with hadn't really changed, but now I accepted him.

As an author, returning to childhood seems to me now like proofing your own work. You've been over it so often you know what's coming. So mostly what you see is what you *think* happened. But every so often something jumps out, you get a fresh perspective and the story changes. And, of course, the place called Longsands in my novel *Purple* owes a lot to my wild-child walks on the beach ...

# IT'S THE JOURNEY THAT COUNTS

*Without contraries is no progression*
— William Blake

My childhood was full of journeys. Some of them were moves and some were visits. It meant that I travelled a lot for a child in the 1950s.

The first big trip was the annual Christmas drive from London to the North East. It took twelve hours through hail and snow with my dad white-knuckling the car around corners like Ahab in a storm. I sat in the back being good. At the end of that drive there was Christmas with family and lights and parties where everyone loved me. It was the kind of journey into darkness where the battle against the elements had a bright-and-shiny ending.

When we returned home it was less edgy, more everyday and ploddy. There were real ups and downs, with threats and scares and school bullies around the corner, but there were also chances to talk with the girls, or to play 'chain tag' in the yard. It wasn't idyllic, but I didn't get 'bashed up' and I had friends on my street. And when we set out in summer on the trip up North I knew I'd be the centre of attention, digging and playing all-hours on the beach.

When I was nine we relocated from London to Sheffield. This was a very different story. London was suburban, Sheffield was tough. We rented a flat near the city centre and I attended a junior school at the top of the hill. The building was black and bunker-like, and the pavement outside was covered with spit marks. It was as if there was a war going on. Once a month, the top class would form up on one side of the playground and the rest would gather opposite. When a boy shouted 'Go!' everyone charged into the middle and beat each other up. Secondary school in Sheffield was worse. One teacher would sit next to a pupil at a desk and jab him repeatedly with a ruler, another pulled boys' hair. I remember the head-master demanding mightily that we all memorised a chapter of Exodus. He was our R.E. teacher but always arrived late to the lesson. On the day of our test, when he required someone to repeat the chapter, I stood up. I'd spent hours learning it by heart but I was shaking so much I couldn't speak.

Outside the classroom, the boys took things further. There were fights and insults and youths calling themselves 'the sex club' who grabbed each other's crotch and exposed themselves in corners. Later, at home I was 'educated' about girls by my cyclist mates. I was told with a grin that what you did was stick it — or that — up her knickers. It seemed so horrible that I decided not to have anything to do with it, ever.

After Sheffield we moved again, this time to a Northumbrian village on the edge of the coalfield. The bullying there was relentless. I didn't have friends, but now I was able to read poetry and walk in the countryside on my own.

Looked at as a narrative, from childhood onward I'd climbed the dramatic arc[1] and reached the top but now, in youth, I'd slipped back to the bottom. Lower than that, because the songs about war and fights in alleyways plus the sexual jokes about milk bottles and keyholes had broken my confidence. I was no good at sport, blushed too often and ducked out of fights. In the game of snakes and ladders I'd slipped off the board. And that was when the inner life, which had always been there, became my chosen journey. On that journey I was able to draw on those painful early experiences to describe my hero learning about what the boys called 'it' in my novel *Purple*.

I shall trace the way of imagination in my next piece, but I still wonder how that other journey, with its fists and abuse, didn't stop me altogether. Maybe the answer's that unless you have problems you don't ask questions.

I don't believe that life is simply about moving on. When we travel, the movement is both outward and inward. We may travel in hope or run in fear. And the arc may be backwards or forwards, or both. Everything's in motion: your mind, your eye, the earth itself. The question is what you make of it.

---

1 According to Freytag's Pyramid, a drama is divided into five parts, or acts which some refer to as a dramatic arc: exposition, rising action, climax, falling action, and dénouement.

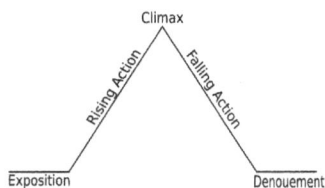

# THE WAY OF IMAGINATION

*All of us have a primitive prompter or commentator within,*
*who from earliest years has been advising us, telling us what*
*the real world is*
— Saul Bellow

*The process of writing is about being given over to something*
*beyond oneself. In this case, the language*
— Paul Muldoon

Picture a room with a boy in bed. The room is small and, though it has a child's wallpaper with rockets and stars and a chest full of toys, it feels quite empty. Bare and untouched, like a cell. It's summer and the glow from the street spreads across the walls. The light is soft and grey, filtered through curtains. Outside, the boys are playing football, shouting; inside, the boy is talking to himself. He's imitating voices — cartoon characters and the woman next door. He speaks with an accent, all la-di-dah. Next he tries cockney. When he imitates children his voice goes squeaky and when he mimics adults he talks into his boots. His impressions are funny.

On the landing, listening at the door, are his parents. They're keeping quiet, enjoying the show. He doesn't know they're there.

The boy is me, or the me I remember. He's the boy who invented stories that he told to his toys. A child alone, sent to bed early, keeping up a patter. A boy whose voice came from nowhere, broadcasting stories from the studio in his head.

When I wrote about it later in a poem called *Their Child is Doing Voices*, I used 'he' instead of 'I'. Writing in third person opened up a space where I could see things more clearly. I began to think about the scene's possible meanings. It was partly the feel — there I was, alone in a room, amusing myself — but also what it stood for. At the time I'd imagined desert islands or 'Invisible Man' exploits tunnelling through walls, but looking back now I realise that it was my first experience of writing.

Here's how:

♪ The empty-but-crowded room is the writer's mind.

♪ The shouts outside are the world at a distance.

♪ The boy's crazy voices are the first drafts going around his head.
♪ The boy's words imitate the world he's cut off from.
♪ It's a monologue, heard by no one.
♪ At the same time, like a diarist in a novel, he suspects deep down that someone's listening.
♪ His parents are those listeners. Their reactions are hidden.
♪ He's also listening to himself, trying to get it right.

So the writer knows, like an actor, that the side of the room he's playing in is cut away. He's alone and he's on stage. Part of him is listening carefully to how it comes across; the other is open to anything. Sometimes he reads out, sometimes he adlibs. He's striking a balance between freedom and constraint.

When I wrote about this incident I added in an approaching thunderstorm. I do remember the hot, humid summers but the storm was poetic licence. So why did I add it?

The purpose was to pack in the hot spots, but also to give a full picture of the times and how it felt, and say something bigger than the facts. I also wanted the flow of tension, building from a distance and ending, quietly, in rain. I was the boy, or the writer, in his own world, waiting for something larger to take over. Of course the experience was intensely subjective. As a child I was very pumped-up. But I hoped the reader would smile at the boy's absurdity while enjoying his ambition to go beyond his physical circumstances.

I do think now that what we do when we write is signpost a pattern. And to do so we have to, as Kurt Vonnegut says, 'Write to please just one person'. My childhood bedroom was one place where I could have it my own way. And that room with its voices, I now realise, was my first taste of facing a blank wall and writing on it. But also, my experience in that room led me to writing about the carving of St Matthew which appears in my novel *Purple*. Seen by my hero on a cathedral wall, the carving shows an angel speaking over the saint's shoulder. The link is that my hero, Matthew Lavender, shares the Evangelist's name — and they are both authors struggling with words in a private-but-public room.

Here is a copy of the poem I wrote:

### Their child is doing voices

It is hot. Outside on the landing his parents
are in readiness, hushed for the show.

Hear him now, stirring.
The whiteness of his mind, at peace, a planet,
is studio enough
where, ice-still in echoes like a deepfreeze mariner,
he inhales to begin.

To preacher-perfect O's mimicking the next doors.
And now the imperatives to weepy Olive Oyl,
hot talk, transmissions, dogfights and now,
waspish, with accent, lisping Daffy Duck,
scolding her charges in squeaky '78.

The window isn't dark. There's a weight outside
of goal calls, tyre yelps, airplays and voices
and, further off, spotlights, flashes, removals
then thunder-heavy hooves drumming to Santa Fé.

So what should we suppose? Whose mind — if anyone's —
keeps him fired up like the all-night swallow
or otherworld explorer pictured on his headboard?
Does he play them, with his dramas, for effect?
And is this a fragment, unintended,
of an endgame still to come?

For him it's just talk. Call signs, signals,
soundings in water. Fragments from the studio
carried in his head. Or deep space sweats
as, enclosed in twilight, he drips out soul.
Those tingling eternals and big bang loops
unwinding through him in long slow burns,
with darkness as backdrop,
squeezed and expectant as a cordial.

One last broadcast and now, in grumbling
double bass, his man's voice, rallying the troops,
ordering to sleep. Then scene change, flashlights,
endplay and whiteness moving closer,
thunder striding floorboards, sparkings, ignitions
and scatterings of applause.

And now just the ghosts, hushed out and tidal,

the air vents sighing, the heartbeat on low, overheard faintly
or suspended to judgement by a long-held breath,
as, sheeted into darkness, his mind runs on forever
to a Mobius strip, with no one there listening
to the first few drops of rain.

# MY SECRET LIFE

*The ego endeavours in all kinds of ways to defend itself against*
*the objective unpleasure and dangers which menace it*
— Anna Freud[1]

My childhood was characterised by solitary play. At an early stage, I crouched by the house with a stick and scraped out the mortar between bricks. Using my thumbs, I filled the holes with a sand-and-water paste. It was my idea of a physical experiment. I'd understood the need for secrecy so I did it on the quiet, when my parents weren't looking. Later I imagined tunnelling out from my bedroom to explore the street as an undercover agent.

Most of my play was like this — quietly subjective, slotting into gaps where people wouldn't see me. So on rainy days the garden shed was my lab, full of paint pots and hoses and strange-shaped implements. It was dark and dusty like a bunker. In there I plotted to take over the world.

Steps behind the shed led up to an overgrown bank. This was my route around to the lawn, squeezing between the fir tree and the shed. I called it my North West Passage. Closing my eyes, I pushed between the wall and the pine needles. I didn't want to see the ghosts hiding in the branches.

I returned to that shed, writing it into my novel *Purple*, but describing its interior through the eyes of Mary, my secondary narrator: 'It was brick-built and square with high-up window-slits, gaps around the doorframe and a hole in the roof. The walls were cobwebbed, plastered one end, and hung with tools on nails. At the back was an old bath full of sea coal. We sat at the front on a large wooden trunk. Beside us there was a box full of kindling and chopped-up logs. The air smelled damp.'

My time playing in that shed gave me what Anna Freud called 'an agreeable fantasy of controlling the world'.[1] In her terms, my ego was using denial to defend itself from vulnerability. It was my safe place, or to put it another way: I was making up a Peter Pan story in which I outflew

1 Freud, A. (1936). The Ego and the Mechanisms of Defence. New York: International Universities Press.

or outfought all the dangers.

In fact most of the dramas were small-scale, but magnified by imagination and seen from more than one angle. So I saw maps in the path and seas in the borders. I looked down on ant lines and beetles and woodlice in corners. But my interest changed to fear when I saw the garden spiders. And after rain I was terrified when the worms came out like an invading army.

Indoors was safer. The games in the house were mental and rule-bound. They included board games and cards where I played both sides, retaking dice throws or pretending I didn't know what cards each player held. In these games, I switched roles, blanking what I knew and changing who I was — it was my own private theatre. Similarly, I'd 'switch' in the mirror, pulling faces and speaking in voices. Or I'd repeat under my breath 'They seek him here, they seek him there', as if I was the Scarlet Pimpernel.

The way I played these games gave me a feeling of being special or unique. I was appearing as the hero in what David Elkind calls the 'personal fable'.[2] My story was all about *me*, written on the wall in invisible ink. And my imaginary audience[3] were inside, watching.

When I was in company, I kept my magic thinking hidden. The boy in the mirror was a very different person from the shy conformist at school. In any case, I wanted to keep myself to myself. There was a secret satisfaction in being so far crazy that no one could read me. But sometimes the 'mad kid' broke out. So at parties I'd go wild, running around shouting and bouncing on beds. And on Christmas Night I hardly slept, appearing very early in the morning white and shaking with anticipation, as if I'd caught a cold.

Solitary play was an escape. It kept me safe, inside myself, but it also cut me off. It was probably so intense because I was an only child. But I think it's still there. So when I dream of fame or argue in advance with someone in my mind or picture what I'd do if *I* ran the country then I know it's my personal fable. Of course now, as an adult, I see it as a habit we all share. It's not so secret and because you've read this piece, the imaginary audience is you.

---

2 The personal fable is the secret story an adolescent invents, casting him/herself as misunderstood hero, with completely unique thoughts and feelings. At the same time, the adolescent believes that everyone else (the imaginary audience) shares the same fascination with her or him as she/he does. Elkind, D (1967). 'Egocentrism in adolescence'.

3 Imaginary audience behavior in children and adolescents. Developmental Psychology, 15(1), 38.

# FOR THE LOSERS

*Accepting failure makes success of life*
— Alan Ginsberg

For many boys, sport is vitally important. For them it's a great outlet and a laugh. It's also a measure of strength and skill and daring and timing. So the top tennis players use a complex mental map of where a ball might go and make split-second adjustments for spin, speed and bounce. Based on experience, the player's coordination between barely-conscious calculation and muscle-reaction is a wonderful dance. And watching or playing sport can be a knife-edge experience where a hair's breadth separates success and failure.

I went to boys' schools where status depended very much on how good or bad you were on the field. It was great for some, but I couldn't run fast or change direction at will. If a ball was in the air I'd drop it, if it was on the ground I'd trip over it and when the team advanced I was the figure lurking at the back trying to avoid contact. So I belonged to the losers.

At the time I felt alone and exposed. I was ashamed of my body and imagined everyone was shouting at me. If they were, it was usually the teachers! As a result I was all over the place. My body felt heavy and my arms and legs wouldn't do what I told them. I tried to hide my fear — so I kept one foot on the bottom while swimming and I ran around the pitch in rugby trying to look vigorous and alert. But my panic showed through. And in the changing room afterwards I was picked on. The bullying undermined me and the next match, of course, was worse again. In sport some people have their shortcomings relentlessly exposed.

But for the people it suits, sport is a character-building activity. It teaches perseverance and working as a team. The fitness it brings can help both body and mind and the individually competitive side may develop into 'running your own race' and breaking records. And there is something beautiful and inspiring about peak performance. It can demonstrate a kind of selfless bravado or what Saul Bellow describes as: 'stillness in the midst of chaos ... something to do with an arrest of attention in the midst of distraction'. So runners sometimes enter what they call the zone, a meditational space where time is suspended and the contest isn't with the opponent but with oneself. And for ordinary joggers (possibly with music in their ears) it can be a floaty experience where they go beyond the limits of everyday life.

But what interests me now, is the losers. I was one, and I feel for the Gareth Southgate anti-hero who takes the blame and has to live with it. Or the backmarker lapped by everyone, who has practised for years only to fail. Losers are more interesting because they have the hardest job. When morale drops and a team is fighting 'the drop' every point is like a tooth extracted. And losers are important not only because the winners need them, but also because it's through adversity that we begin to reflect. When the going gets tough we start to ask questions.

Of course there are ways of covering up. So Matthew, the youthful protagonist in my coming-of-age novel *Purple*, tries to hide his sense of being 'out of it' behind a cooler-than-thou mask. Some boys use humour to 'keep their end up', others gain respect by finding a specialist role on the field and others become experts in the stats and history of their chosen team. But for the persistent losers like me the effort went elsewhere, into dreams and reading and playing chess, and the badge of loser became a mark of pride and difference, and hidden feelings of superiority.

Of course losing in sport is often through no fault of one's own. Injury or accident can keep a sports star out for years, and it takes a particular mental toughness to come back, or to know when to quit. It's often through pain and loss that we discover our true selves. So losers are an example to us all. They show us how to adjust to the restrictions of our time-limited, vulnerable existence. Their injuries remind us of age and infirmity. Their depressions and collapses are part of the human condition. And their misfortunes, given proper attention, can make us more compassionate towards others when things go wrong. There's a loser somewhere in all of us; the trick is to acknowledge it.

# THE DARK SIDE

*Like one, that on a lonesome road / Doth walk in fear and dread,
/ And having once turned round walks on, / And turns no more
his head; / Because he knows, a frightful fiend / Doth close
behind him tread*
— Coleridge

I've always been afraid of the dark. As a child I crept across the landing
with fists ready to fight off ghosts. In the bathroom I was menaced by
mini-devils who jumped out of sight whichever way I turned. I remember
lying awake listening to *The Quatermass Experiment* on TV. I was four at
the time and I'd glimpsed the shots of the crashed spaceship before being
sent to bed. Imagining the story and hearing weird music rising from
below was almost worse than seeing the programme itself.

In bed I slept with the pillow over my head to block out the dark. If
criminals or monsters were sneaking up on me, I didn't want to know.
Even today, if I get up in the night, I sometimes imagine I'm being watched
or followed. And when I'm alone I sleep with the door open and the
landing light on.

According to Freud, fear of the dark results from separation anxiety
disorder (SAD).[1] The child is afraid that a much-loved place or
person, often a mother, will be taken away. I think in my case separation
anxiety was a symptom of an era where war was the norm and children
were evacuated. It showed itself in hospital rules about feeding babies,
resulting in a battle between my mother's attempts to feed by the clock
and my demands for more. I have pictures showing how thin we both
became.

I remember having other anxiety symptoms as a child. So I dreamed of
contracting a life-threatening illness and being rushed into hospital. Closing my eyes, I saw myself lying there with my chastened parents gazing at

---

1. Freud, Sigmund (1916). Introduction to Psychoanalysis: 'I once heard a child
who was afraid of the darkness call out: "Auntie, talk to me, I'm frightened." "But
what good will that do? You can't see me," to which the child replied: "If someone
talks, it gets lighter."'

me in a state of shock. It was my revenge — they'd not believed the signs, now they *had* to listen. I forgave them, of course, and pictured my homecoming, where I was treated like royalty. So I lay in bed and feasted on cake and fizzy drinks and strawberry ice cream. My imaginary timeout continued with weeks off school, followed by a return on crutches or in a wheelchair with my classmates smiling nicely and being extra-kind because 'you can't hit a man when he's down'.

I also dreamed of being captured by boys on the way home from school. They grabbed me, frogmarched me to the waste ground and tied me to a tree. After a long night I was rescued by the police, questioned and exonerated. My parents were horrified, the bully boys were found out and I was awarded a medal for bravery.

My fears were often ambivalent. For instance, I was afraid of climbing into the water at the swimming baths but loved the sea. On holiday I'd wade out waist-high and splash and jump, or I'd float on my tummy in the shallows. I loved the wild freedom of the sea but I never learned to swim. I had a similar love-hate attitude to spiders, shivering as I watched their fat black-and-yellow bodies fixed like jewels in the centre of webs. And as I grew older, my own body became increasingly fascinating and ugly. So I kept myself covered, using the excuse that my skin burned easily, and I chose to walk alone in the countryside, where no one would see me.

The final 'dark' experience was an attempt, at Halloween, to confront my fears. I'd been reading Shelley, in *Alastor*, describing how: *I have made my bed / In charnels and on coffins, where black death / Keeps record of the trophies won from thee.* I was excited and wanted to imitate his daring. This might bring me secret knowledge.

So I slipped out of the house at midnight using my key and crept around to the local graveyard. My chest was tight and my teeth were chattering but I forced myself through the gate then stopped dead, thinking I heard a noise. It was high and weird like the music I'd heard during *Quatermass*. It sounded half-human, half-animal and dangerously supernatural. I turned and ran, only slowing when I reached a safe distance. When I sneaked into the house I slipped into bed and put my head beneath the pillow.

I didn't challenge the dark again.

*Language is analytical, with defined meanings and a grammar of connections. This makes reading a practised skill like hitting a ball or riding a bike.*

*As an author I don't have a camera to show you what it's like so I have to build up a picture bit by bit, choosing what I focus on.*

*Starting a novel by 'grabbing' the reader is like beginning a song on top C: there's nowhere left to go.*

# 4th MOVEMENT

## CROSS-DRESSING

**What readers said about:**

My Outing                    A Dream

Incognito                    Dressing Up

and

My Story

My grandad's cross-dressing in the 40s/50s was my family's shameful secret. Sadly my grandad died before I was born, but I glimpsed the struggle he must have faced in this beautifully honest & emotive piece. The sweet use of imagery in *A Dream* was a particularly touching moment of self-awareness & a quest for freedom. It's so easy to forget that a life choice most of us consider 'cool, interesting & expressive' could ever have had such a dangerous negativity surrounding it.

— *Julie Williams, Singer/Songwriter.*

I particularly like the sense of mystery in the dream story of Jenny with the ripe bobble hat. The image of the blackberry made me think of large breasts and nipples and feminine sensuality and then it felt all too real when she couldn't handle the boy's acting and she turned cold and rejected his sensuality, leaving him crying with shame in the act of showing her his vulnerability.

When I work as a counsellor (positively, neutrally, joyfully!) with cross-dressing and trans issues, I ask clients (couples or individuals) to tell me stories and dreams they have had linked to sexuality. I feel it is often right to narratise like this for several reasons: one to preserve privacy and to avoid evoking shame and secondly working in narrative is the way that I understand better and can start to make an imaginative bridge with clients. Narratising is an externalising that frees the client to release more material, including the pre-conscious stuff, bypassing the frontal lobes and allowing the primitive brain/wisdom to free itself. I liked the way the writing brought in some theory and even the bullet points seemed to flow quite naturally. That's interesting. Shows how genre fluidity is bringing forth interesting new genres.

— *Barbara Bloomfield, Counselling Supervisor; Journalist and Writer with five published books.*

My goodness this is such good writing. What Leslie Tate does is lay himself emotionally open and honest in a manner that cannot fail to touch the heart of the reader.

If I'm honest, I'm not usually especially interested in autobiographical writing, but Leslie Tate has inspired me to read more if it is to be of this quality. *Heaven's Rage* and the chapter I read, *Cross-Dressing*, is raw, beautifully written and utterly compelling reading. When I'd finished reading *Cross-Dressing* I wanted to reach out my arms to Leslie Tate and hold him close.

Anyone who has struggled with their sexual and personal identity will find so much that resonates here and for those of us who have always been conventional, Leslie Tate illustrates what others have had to contend with. That's not to say that this is a sympathy requesting piece. Far from it. It is a true, moving and fascinating account of how Leslie began cross-dressing and how he was viewed, and viewed himself, as a result. It explores the way the media treats those who appear other, the way society expects certain norms for acceptance and how hard so many of us find it to be easy in our own skin.

What I enjoyed most about this piece was the eloquence of the writing. Leslie Tate has a beautiful turn of phrase that conveys perfectly the emotions of the moment. He presented me with concepts that had never really reached my consciousness and made me think in a manner I found hugely skilful.

No matter what your own personal viewpoint and perspective, *Cross-Dressing* cannot fail to move and impress the reader. It's magnificent.
— *Linda Hill, Editor Linda's Book Bag; Best Book Review Blog Award 2016.*

Leslie Tate's piece is exceptional, riveting, and writing at its most distinctive. Exploring as he does his public outing as a teacher in the early 1980s he takes us on a fascinating journey where we sit listening as he whispers it in our ear as though he were our close friend or neighbour, making it special, wonderful, something to be celebrated. And this is contrasted admirably by his description of his early years wrapped in the struggle of coming to terms with his identity. We share his painful secrecy, living through a time, as he did, when it was sinful to deviate from the so-called norm, but are led to enjoy his positive, witty but analytical expose of himself — all of himself. How many of us dare do that? And with such vibrant literary talent. So this is not just a piece about one person's journey of liberation, of his continuing self-realisation both through cross dressing, and as a writer, this is a universal challenge to prejudice. Few pieces of writing have moved me as much as this did: everyone must read it.
— *Neil Beardmore, Dramatist, Author, Poet, Artist and Musician.*

Compelling, moving and beautiful.
— *Mark Crane, Artistic Director at Theatre on Wax.*

## A Reader's Transgender Story

I cannot complain about my childhood, I suppose it could have been better but it could also have been very much worse. I was the second of six children which meant a few extra responsibilities but also a fair amount of freedom. We lived in our own semi-det house on a nice estate and watched the massive council estate being built at the end of our road — it swallowed many acres of allotments and fields and was well over a mile square. This provided me and my young friends with lots of adventures — I was particularly skinny with round NHS specs and the innocent look of the Milky Bar kid so I got away with all sorts of petty crimes. Nightly raids were made to collect workmen's Corona bottles and claim the deposits back — it was a good earner even between three of us.

On the one hand I could be very adventurous and lead my gang into fights with the new kids on the estate but I was also the gentle brother who would spend ages teasing the knots out of my two sisters' hair — they would literally plead for me to be allowed to do their hair and I loved creating new and pretty styles for them. I showed absolutely no flair for sport except for running and even then I was told that I ran like a girl. Oh how often was I told that I behaved more like a girl. Little did they know that I often thought and felt like one too.

My survival depended to a large extent on bluff and bluster. I learnt not to run away from bullies but to make sure they hurt their fists so much that they didn't fancy a re-run. Most girls seemed to instinctively know that I was one of them — I even ended up in their team for kiss chase — although they had to do all the kissing. The local boys were very forward for their age, probably due to being cramped up in tiny houses with many kids and possibly sharing rooms with older brothers or sisters and their boyfriends etc. By contrast I knew nothing about sex — when I imagined being naked with a girl I would dream of a sensual experience not unlike a lesbian affair. When puberty struck I thought I was going to die — I had my first experience of full-on gender dysphoria. I looked down in the bath and panic struck me. I really wondered what had gone wrong with me.

Around the same time I was mooching around with my friends after spending their pocket money in the local shopping precinct when one of them noticed a black lacy garment lying in the road. It may have been dropped out of a laundry bag or been lost by one of the many courting couples that parked there at night. Either way it was now mine and I made some pretext for looking after it. It was a beautiful black lacy Berlei bra — before long I was alone in my bedroom — as I sneaked it out of my pocket it released a delicious fragrance or perfume that drove my senses wild. In a flash my cotton vest was off and I had soon mastered the straps to achieve a perfect fit. I recall standing in front of the mirror to see my lightly-tanned face flushed with excitement — the contrast of that delectable item against my slim hairless body. Sun bleached hair and my NHS specs — oh the specs had to go!! Before long my secret bra was teamed with a pretty pair of knickers and I had found my alter ego.

— *Melissa Maine.*

# MY OUTING

During the 1983 Bermondsey by-election, the British press, tiring of their daily homophobic attacks on Peter Tatchell, picked up an article I wrote in the sexual politics section of a small but influential left-wing Labour journal. The article was about how I believed that cross-dressing challenged conventional ideas of masculinity. It included a picture of me in a dress.

The journalists seized on my story, passing it around and featuring me on the inside page of nearly every single newspaper, printing my name, the street I lived in and where I worked. The 'family friendly' *Daily Mail* reporter went further, ringing up my house, pretending to be a social worker, and asking my first wife how she felt about the damage I was supposedly doing to our children.

My story ran for ten days as the papers decided when to use my so-called 'confessional' to fill a vacant column. There was no 'public interest' justification for picking on me, I didn't hold public office and I hadn't committed a crime, I was an active constituency member of the Labour Party and that was enough for their purposes.

When *The Sun* printed my story I was 'outed' in front of the students at the London secondary school where I taught. It was the fourth day in 'my story' and I'd already been questioned by a few kids who'd got wind of something, but being on page three in the most-read British newspaper guaranteed wall-to-wall notoriety. Realising I'd nowhere to go to, the apocalyptic words of the song *Sinner Man* ran through my head as I walked into school with 2,000 pairs of eyes trained on me — or that's how it felt. They were leaning out of windows and gathering at the doors, awaiting my arrival, curious to see how I looked. To be honest, most of that was in my head, but I knew they expected a dramatic entrance. Maybe I'd roll up as a drag queen, tiptoe in as a flower fairy, or appear in assembly as a panto dame? Certainly, my status had changed. From now on I would be scrutinised for tell-tale 'signs' — my hair length, my fingernails, the pitch of my voice, the way I walked — and if I didn't give them cause then I was in hiding, guilty of a crime I'd tried to cover up.

Coming out was a shock. It was as if I'd become a character in a TV exposé. It felt like I was see-through, held up as something 'other', and my day clothes — male, of course — couldn't hide me. I no longer possessed my own story, I'd become the property of the Press, talked about and ridiculed and subject to false witness, so that the person I'd been no longer existed. My humanity had been brought into question. I was the sum of a number of derogatory terms, including 'weirdo', 'transvestite', 'deviant' and 'public enemy'.

That first day at school I went in blind. I didn't quote my right to silence or claim mistaken identity but I did hold out a hope that it might blow over. And at first there was a lull. My own classes refused to believe it. They didn't want me 'like that', and since they didn't ask I didn't have to tell. They still respected me and I preferred it that way. I felt like the captain of a ship surrounded by storms who keeps a quiet light burning on deck.

But on the corridor I was stared at by girls and avoided by boys who turned and flattened themselves against the wall as if I might carry a dangerous disease. The boys were particularly reactive. Behind my back they sniggered or guffawed or muttered darkly, 'bums against the wall lads'. Others who were busy or not bothered walked past ignoring me, while some, usually girls, stepped up and asked quietly, 'Why do you want to do that, sir?'

I soon came to realise that their sympathy, however well-intentioned, wasn't what it seemed. They weren't interested in learning about cross-dressing, what they wanted to know was 'why do that *at all?*' and, ultimately, 'Why can't you stop it?'

I found my reply. It's still with me today as the beginning of my story. I didn't try to offer theories, describe my experiences, or talk them through the long history of trans people. When they asked me, 'Why do you want to do that, sir?' I simply answered 'Why not?'

# A DREAM

It began with a dream where I found myself alone in the woods. I'd been captured by a gang on the way to school and tied to a tree in what people called the wasteland. The boys had been cruel but I'd been brave, and now they'd left me the ropes didn't hurt. I was by myself in a world of soft leaves, warm sun and cool, gentle feelings. I could watch for animals and listen to the birds. It was as if I'd always been there.

A song went through my head: *If you go down to the woods today, you're sure of a big surprise. If you go down to the woods today, you'd better go in disguise.*

The song continued, cutting off at the words: *But safer to stay at home.*

Realising how I must look, I was glad no one could see me. And yet I was happy to be alive and in the open air. My limbs were tingling and my breath was short. Looking up, I could see the clouds as islands in the sky. I was a child awaiting rescue, feeling free, comfortable, attractive, relieved to be myself.

In my dream I was thinking about the times I'd walked home with Jenny, the girl at number 43. She was my age, small and dark, and usually walked ahead, speaking unexpectedly, and sometimes laughing when I clowned or said something silly. Her back was straight, her uniform was neat, her face was serious and she wore a beret. I thought she was rather like me.

The beret was green with a soft, black bobble on top that wobbled as she walked. It looked like a ripe blackberry. I wanted to know how it felt and how it stayed on and suddenly, without thinking, my hand shot out and lifted the bobble. The cap came with it.

"That's mine," I said, trying it on my head, thinking she'd laugh.

"Give it back," she said, not turning.

"Mine."

Jenny ignored me.

"It's here," I said, placing her cap on a wall.

She looked back.

"You have to get it," I called.

Jenny shook her head.

"Come on ..."

"No," she said, pressing on.

I began to weaken, "Just stop."

Jenny kept going.

"Stop."

Still she walked.

"You can have it," I called out, blushing.

Jenny turned.

"Look," I shouted, pointing back to where I'd left it. "It's yours."

Slowly and deliberately, she shook her head.

"Yours," I repeated, jiggling about.

"You'll be in trouble," she said, moving towards her gate.

"No," I cried.

"I'll tell," she said darkly, stepping through to the path.

Realising she meant it, I turned. "Wait," I cried, running back, hot-foot and breathless, to pick up her cap. When I returned, Jenny was there, standing quietly just inside her gate. Feeling stupid, I handed it over. "Take it," I said, fighting back tears.

She'd won, I'd been a fool, and when she took it I was crying. The last thing I remember was her superior smile as she glanced back at me and took the cap indoors, holding it by the bobble. With it went my shame.

Back in the woods I was by myself. The air felt cool and the sun was going down. I was picturing Jenny and wondering what she'd say. The boys had mocked me and left me on display. I was there on my own, looking quite different. Though I knew what they'd done, I needed to look down to be sure. When I did, I was happy. I was myself, calmly comfortable, elaborately done up and fully protected. It felt quite special.

I was dressed as a girl.

# INCOGNITO

I kept my cross-dressing secret, and didn't tell anyone. I'd read about cat burglars who came and went in silence and removed a photo or ring or page from a diary, and like them I tiptoed into bedrooms and sneaked things out of drawers in a house that wasn't mine. I was on high alert, rehearsing my lines. If anyone found me, I'd tell them my intentions were good, that I'd fought back my urges and kept myself intact for as long as I could. In any case, I'd say, I'd been curious and not really meant it, this was my first time, a once-only trial.

My head was full of stories where I held out on my own, playing for time. I'd cast myself as a loner, a survivor, moving through darkness while outwardly I was the shy boy who smiled and waved from the window. Nobody could fault me or see what I was up to, and like Scheherazade I had my story ready. I was incognito; invisible, even to myself. And because I was nameless, nothing could touch me.

\*\*\*

I remember working hard at becoming like my dad. He was tall and lean and had trained himself to be sporty, using his mind to calculate a ball's flight, talking about googlies and yorkers. On our beach holidays he could hurl a stick out into the waves, way beyond where our dog could swim. I was surprised by the sudden violence exploding from his arm when he leaned back and chucked it. All the men on the beach threw like that: hard and fast, directing their balls like missiles. They laughed about it afterwards while listening to the cricket on the radio. It seemed odd that when a bouncer hit a batsman they were outraged, demanding that the bowler be sent off. And they argued over theories about who should bat next, the other side's weakness and what they'd do as captain.

My dad didn't say much, but when he did he seemed to have the answer. As a commentator and occasional player, he took his sport seriously. So, when I asked about bowling, he took me to a private, walled-in area, chalked up some stumps, and tried to coach me. From then on I practised for hours on my own, running up and wheeling my arm to flight the ball and land 'on the spot'. But I didn't have much grip and when I bowled, the ball was short or long or wide of the mark and he swatted me to the boundary.

As I got older, we took long walks together and worked in the garden with him digging out stones, sweating like a navvy, while I wheeled them off in barrows. The garden project, like most of his handyman activities, was forever on the go. As soon as he'd levelled one lawn and planted some roses we moved house and the digging and the sweating began again. By the third garden he seemed to have had enough, talking about 'struggling', being 'exhausted' and 'just plodding on'.

When his gardening became a one-man contest my interest switched to playing him at chess. He'd taught me, he was a keen amateur and we played most nights. My dad's style was *never say die*, he'd sacrifice his pieces for show then stonewall doggedly, hanging on till bedtime cut things short. When I became good enough to compete at county level and then for my country, he gave up the contest, switching to proud dad and supporter.

In the end my efforts to follow in his footsteps didn't work. Being male through sport or strength or physical endurance or 'holding up my end' when the men began joshing wasn't for me. What strength I had was mental.

\*\*\*

I continued cross-dressing in absolute secrecy right through youth. Looking back now and drawing on Deception Theory,[1] I can identify three main strategies I used to avoid detection:

1. *Instrumental*: to avoid punishment or to protect resources.
2. *Relational*: to maintain relationships or bonds.
3. *Identity*: to preserve 'face' or self-image.

With these three I could keep up appearances and throw my opponents off the scent. In terms of the theory I made myself:

1. Sensible, practical, down-to-earth, rolling up my sleeves to focus on getting things done.
2. Nicey-nicey, ultra-attentive and above all suspicion.
3. Priest-like, focused on matters of importance and higher things.

On the chessboard, my dad had always told me, I needed a battle plan. In war, he said, you must look for the opening, engage your target and keep 'em guessing. So I played against the world, laying false trails and feigning

---

1 Buller D.B. & Burgoon, J.K. (1996). Interpersonal deception theory. Communication Theory. 6 (3): 203–242.

innocence. I had my openings, my defence was near-perfect, and I carried it off so nothing showed. I was wild and clever and daringly 'different' — and that gave me the upper hand.

Through looking ahead and plotting my moves, I kept my secret. I had it all covered, and no one suspected. And each day I got by without detection was another point to me. The people 'out there' were my opponents; they couldn't see my desires or detect what I was thinking, and behind my mask I was safe, half-female, half-male and able to outsmart them all ...

# DRESSING UP

In the *Rhyme of the Ancient Mariner*, the mariner touches the shoulder of the wedding guest, beginning his story with "There was a ship." When the wedding guest objects, the mariner hypnotises his unwilling subject with a fixed and glittering stare.

Using a similar but much lighter technique, the great master of hypnotherapy, Milton H. Erickson, developed the 'handshake induction'[1] designed to produce a gentle trance. Erickson would distract his client at the start of a consultation by gradually withdrawing his hand and touching the wrist so gently that his subject couldn't quite tell when the contact ended.

In both cases the goal was for the subject to pay attention to hints and suggestions normally passed over, and focus uncritically on a single train of thought. In the process, the subject would discover hidden truths about the self or personal experience.

The story of my cross-dressing was similar.

It developed from an 'interrupted move' — the dream-feel of a dress worn in a wood — and the long-term memory (still with me today) of heightened flow and wellbeing. Dressed up, I was nicer, fuller, more glamorous and in touch. I'd come across something special, I was fascinated, and wanted more.

After that there were whispers, voices in my head telling me to try it, to go back to the wood, do what I liked and find out where it led ...

Years later, having been outed by the papers, I was on the corridor of a London Comprehensive saying, "Why not?" to a girl who'd asked me to explain. I was married, with children, I was political, educated and a survivor-teacher. My reply was intended as a challenge, turning the tables, but in some secret part of me I understood what she meant.

From the start I'd called it my own *funny habit*. There were various 'explanations', words and phrases I'd used in my internal arguments and struggles not to 'do it' — it didn't have to touch me, I was going through a phase, it was nothing really, an act I'd developed and really wasn't me. I'd

---

1 Milton H. Erickson & Ernest L. Rossi Hypnotic Realities, ISBN 0-8290-0112-3.

reasoned and protested, tried bullying myself, but ended giving in. And the habit became obsessive, beginning with a petticoat taken from a drawer, a small piece I liked and viewed in the mirror like a woman in a shop, then all sorts of underwear with skirts and blouses, squeezing into heels. That was when the house was empty, 'going the full way' when my parents were out shopping. More often I tiptoed across the landing to sneak-thief an item and take it back to bed. In the dark I was hidden, I'd a girl in there with me, I was lucky to have her and no one could touch us. And afterwards, when I ghost-walked the carpet to return my item, I prayed my parents wouldn't hear me.

In fact I prayed quite a lot when they were out, splitting myself into angel and devil and getting red-faced and loud, pleading for the strength not to do it. I was in the danger zone, the route ahead was dark, but a Faustian curiosity drove me on. Looking back now, I can feel the loneliness. This was unheard-of, I'd no points of reference and, like the mariner, the weight of my secret marked me out.

I was lucky not to get caught. Aversion therapy, using pictures and electric shocks, was the 'treatment' at the time. It only took one item misplaced or a tell-tale stain, and the questioning would begin. So although it didn't happen, I've a film in my head of my parents' disbelief, their shock and disgust, the hospital visits and the silence that would follow.

Later I discovered Robert Stoller's ideas of primary femininity,[2] and the long history of transgendered people, but I still knew when I answered the challenges at school that wearing women's clothes had its stigma. Films like *Psycho* had made sure of that. At best it was considered silly, a kind of regrettable, narcissistic, pumped-up self-indulgence. "Is it really necessary?" was the question behind what I'd been asked. And the girl had asked it in a tone that brought back my parents saying "That's not really like you." There were other voices too: cynical colleagues who saw me as naïve, that I'd given the press their story, so what did I expect? Or puzzled, well-meaning friends who were worried, advising caution with world-weary smiles. Then there was the voice of social responsibility: what about my children, how did they feel, and did my wife really let me do that? The finger was pointing and I was to blame.

At school I didn't talk about history or respecting choices or understanding difference. I couldn't really. It wasn't straightforward, there were so many stereotypes, and time was too short. And like an actor in the spotlight I had to play my part, be authoritative and deliver my lines. But

2 Stoller, Robert (1968). Sex and Gender: On the Development of Masculinity and Femininity, Science House, New York City.

in hindsight, if I had to explain, speaking as my own advocate, this is what I'd say:

♪ Cross-dressing is part of a spectrum, it has its own place and belongs to the rainbow.

♪ It's a trance state, and involuntary.

♪ At the same time it's a ritual, a surrender, a deliberate giving way — what Gill and Brenman call 'regression in the service of the ego'.

♪ Acting through the body, it changes the mind.

♪ Ignored, it piles up the pressure. Accepted, it has healing properties.

♪ For me it has become easier, more comfortable, just something I do.

♪ It has helped me to understand questions of difference and exclusion, and our common humanity.

♪ We all have our conditions, our quirks, our off-beat and funny ways ...

So why not enjoy it?

# MY STORY

When the British press 'outed' me they chose not to cover my real story. They could have asked about my childhood or the years in the closet, they could have invited me to explain or quoted my article, they could even have taken an interest in how I'd changed and who I'd become; instead they lampooned me as a 'self-confessed transvestite' and 'Labour extremist', who shouldn't be teaching in a school.

Of course, a human-interest story wouldn't have suited their purposes. They wanted a cautionary tale about people in left-wing groups to amuse and scare their readers. 'Don't go there!' they were saying, pointing at me. I was their shadow side, *the enemy within*, an example of why it was better to project, act tough and not let down the barriers. Because of course, we're all on the spectrum.

My story began with leaving university and setting up home with another teacher. I imagined that getting married and having children would be my introduction to what the world called 'maturity'. And for a while, it seemed I might indeed be able to ignore my urges. I also had a belief that an awareness of the past would keep me 'in the clear'. To stay in touch but not act out, I told myself, was nine-tenths of the battle.

At another level, I probably realised that my mind games wouldn't work. Despite the ever-present risk of discovery, I'd been cross-dressing for 20+ years, so it had to go deep. In the words of an old song it had 'got a hold on me' — and that made it dangerous and hard to handle.

From the start I'd been a reactive child, so when I 'dressed' I'd shake and go weak and be all of a flutter. I was at the mercy of this other, secret self. Suddenly I was lit up, warm and see-through like a butterfly in the sun. But as time went on, my sessions became more lurid, dressing and ogling in the mirror then gradually stripping off and acting like a vamp.

But then I reached a point where I told myself I'd outgrown all that.

So, in the first flush of marriage, although I was tempted, I managed not to touch my first wife's clothes. Instead I told myself that being affectionate was enough to satisfy my 'feminine side' and therefore I didn't need to do it. But as the marriage became more difficult, my 'dressing' returned, though the feel was rather different. By now, as an experienced man, I didn't believe in guilt or shame, but I still felt too raw and inexperienced to be seen, so I dressed in private and got it over quickly, keeping a distance between self and behaviour — and my habit remained nameless, and no part of me.

Then I started drinking. I saw alcohol as a lifeline, giving me the strength to get through the day. Part of the problem was that I wanted to write, and work stood in the way, but also I'd always been tired, with headaches and fatigue, and teaching compounded the problem. In the classroom I could carry off the act, and the pupils respected me, but in the evening I was exhausted. So I needed a pick-me-up, something stronger to get me through.

For a while, I used drink as an extension of myself. So I went all evening topping up my glass, aiming to maintain my high at just the right level. That was what I told myself, but in reality by late evening I'd lost all control. My warm, helpful glow had become an inflationary blur that softened everything, making me feel both collapsed and larger than life. I remember promising myself that I'd use this experience as material for my writing, and imagining my name bracketed with Dylan Thomas and Malcolm Lowry. But I could barely stand, and next morning my body ached all over. Effectively, I'd exchanged one kind of exhaustion for another. And in that condition anything extra, like writing, was out of the question.

So why did I do it?

♪ I was living the highs and lows of alcohol, seeing how far I could go, while trying not to look where the drink was taking me.

♪ This was my story, proving I was alive.

♪ I believed it was unique to me, a challenge I had to rise to.

♪ It took me out of the ordinary, the humdrum, the everyday.

♪ I knew, deep down, it was a death wish.

When my first wife urged me to see the doctor, I put it off for a while, but ended booking an appointment. I went along expecting nothing, until my doctor asked me if I was hiding something. His question, delivered gently without a hint of disapproval, made me realise it was time I talked.

Telling him I cross-dressed was my first open declaration. I thought he might write it down then pass on to other things but to my surprise he wanted to know more. After listening, he advised me that it wasn't that unusual and that I should speak to my wife. I left the surgery feeling stirred up. Everything I'd locked up inside me was suddenly rising to the surface. What I was about to say would expose me and there'd be no going back. Fortunately, my wife was more relieved than shocked. She told me 'If that's all it was,' I must dress like that and bought me some women's clothes. That was when things began to change.

I didn't stop drinking straightaway. It wasn't till a year later, after several failed attempts, including phone calls and counselling and a visit to Alcoholics Anonymous, that I got up one morning, looked in the mirror, and realised it was over. That day, for the first time, I used the word alcoholic, telling my wife that I intended to give up. Of course I had to prove it with a period of abstinence but my resolution held and eventually I went public, declaring my problem and asking my friends to help me stay dry. So the talk with the doctor had helped. He'd taken me seriously, which I'd not expected, and offered an opinion that what I'd been hiding wasn't so unusual – and he'd done it calmly, without talking down. Listening to him, I realised that I wasn't such an oddity after all. His words set off a process that changed my habits and my views on gender, leading to health, renewal and, of course, being outed by the papers.

After speaking to my first wife and the doctor I started wearing women's clothes at home. In the safety of the house I wore long skirts and blouses and practical shoes. The women I admired weren't that glam so I didn't use make-up or wigs, preferring to appear as a man in a dress. Of course I felt odd, but I carried it off by giving the impression that nothing much had changed. In truth, I was hiding my doubts behind a smile. It was like stepping out on stage, unprepared, with no idea of what I was going to say.

So I didn't get too 'done up' at home, mainly because I loved my children and didn't want to upset them. The message was: 'I'm still your dad'. But although I cross-dressed with family and friends, I was still shy around windows and hung back when someone came to the door. Sometimes I had to change in a rush and pack away the clothes in order to avoid discovery. Although I felt happier in myself, it wasn't easy to wear women's clothes and remain invisible.

But when the papers featured me I was forced into the open. So I began going out cross-dressed, though in ways that reduced the risk, working out my route in advance and driving after dark. It still felt dangerous walking to and from the carpark, but very few people seemed to notice. I went to political meetings using a long poncho to cover my clothes and attended parties wearing earrings and heels – putting on a show, dancing wildly and getting into arguments when people made snide comments. I joined the gay movement, learning that being 'out' is a continuous effort, and on Pride days I demonstrated. I remember travelling to a transvestite/transsexual pub in Islington and not feeling comfortable because of the emphasis on glamour and the pressure to 'go the full way' and have an operation. I think being trans today is much more open to individual variation. It might seem that 'passing' as a woman, though difficult to achieve, is rather safer than being identifiably *in between* like Eddie Izzard. But whatever you do word gets out. And of course I know of friends who have been violently pursued, threatened, shunned, ostracised and abused. I was lucky enough not to lose my home, job or relationship and that my mother didn't find out!

Looking back now, my story doesn't feel as dramatic as it seemed at the time. As an author I'm interested in the whole range of human behaviour and what I went through was a fairly solitary experience. It tested me, I was fortunate not to be 'found out' until later in life but now it sits quite comfortably on me. And I know it's important because it feeds into my writing and it has helped me to grow.

*Reading one page will tell you a lot more about a book than any synopsis.*

*Starting a book is difficult: there are so many things to establish. Easy-to-read starts often lead to thin, under-pressured writing.*

*Plot emerges naturally, riskily, unexpectedly from style and vocabulary.*

# 5th MOVEMENT

## BOOKS, WRITING &
## CREATIVE MEMORY

**What readers said about:**

| | |
|---|---|
| *A Book is an Adventure* | *Stories Lead to Stories* |
| *Not the Death of the Author* | *My Imaginary Autobiography* |
| *Getting the Gist of It* | *Memory* |
| *Feeling for the Past* | *The Time of Trial* |

and
*Wrestling with my Angel*

I really enjoyed the chapter and felt it was part of a book that was important and had new and very personal and brave things to say. I thoroughly enjoyed the read and, though I don't know Leslie at all, felt I had got to know something — more than that, a lot — about his life. The writing really opened doors and windows and widened those cracks through which — as Leonard Cohen says — the light gets in.
— *John MacKenna, Playwright, Novelist and Poet, Winner of the Hennessy Literary Award, the Irish Times Fiction Award and the C Day-Lewis Award.*

'Writing, for me, is like wriggling into a hiding place through a narrow entrance.' With these words we are pulled into some small, dark spaces, into the world of childhood memory, the bridge into adulthood, and into detailed descriptions of writing routines. The writing is tactile, intimate and always my response is visceral. I am all the richer for reading it.
— *Katie Willis, finalist the Puffin Review Fairy Tale Competition. Anthologised in Flamingo Land: And Other Stories.*

Reading this reminded me of two other stories: the King Midas myth and *The Monkey's Paw* by W.W. Jacobs. The moral here is 'Be careful what you wish for, you may get it'. I am still pondering Leslie Tate's Jungian interpretation of the wish fulfilment stories as addiction. Could it be that a strong craving or addiction sets human nature out of balance, so things have to happen to show the addict that

they need to change their behaviour and restore natural balance? In so many things, yin and yang, darkness and light counterbalance.
— *Jill Hipson, BSL Teacher, BA Hons in English Literature.*

# A BOOK IS AN ADVENTURE

I remember reading Arthur Ransome's *Swallows and Amazons* and imagining the book's setting as a vaguely-defined territory inside me. I'd never heard of The Lake District so I invented the location as I read, ignoring the references to farmers and charcoal burners and other aspects of Lakeland life. I was entranced by the children's freedom, so I set their adventures in the only place that felt the same – around sand dunes beside the sea. In my mind, the Walker children were desert island castaways and a lake the size of Windermere could only be equalled by the sea.

I acted out my version of *Swallows and Amazons* when we went to stay with my grandparents at the seaside. Behind the dunes there were clumps of sea buckthorn with hidden tunnels where I crawled, casting myself as a pirate. I sneaked along the back alleyways between houses to outflank The Amazons. And when I walked the front I followed strangers who I suspected were in league with Captain Flint.

So I wrote my favourite story into the world. It was a reversal of the 'notebook approach' where an author uses and adapts personal experience. This was the book reworking life.

I was similarly entranced by the articles and pictures in Arthur Mee's *Children's Encyclopaedia*. Reading its jumble of scientific inventions, myths, epic journeys and tipping points in history (with a considerable bias towards the British Empire) I formed a patchwork picture of an imaginary zone full of strange events and surprising information. It was a country of the mind with full-colour plates of dinosaurs, pyramids, knights in armour and rockets taking off. In this case the delights of reading were superior to anything life could offer. This was a documentary introduction to the wonders of the world.

Reading *Alice in Wonderland* brought craziness into my life. This was the land of upside-down and topsy-turvy. An impossible out-of-kilter adventure which could turn anything into its polar opposite. So as I walked the streets a hole could open up, a cat on a fence might wink at me, I could be suddenly taller than the sky, or shrunken to the size of a mouse. The laws of physics were suspended and, for a moment, anything was possible. This was my imagination taking flight into the realm of the Puer Eternis – the Peter Pan boy who soared over the heads of everyone.

Later still, when I read the M.L. James ghost story *Oh Whistle And I'll Come To You My Lad*, the unreal became an ever-present threat. In the story the malevolent force never fully shows itself but attacks inside sheets. As a result I came to question everything I could see. If sheets could become hideouts for dark forces then my protected life was suddenly a sham. Ordinary objects had a dangerous inner nature which couldn't be predicted. Nothing was as it seemed.

To me, these books seem to illustrate four different types of reading experience. The first reshapes the world, the second uses a documentary framework, the third puts the reader's mind at the centre of the action and the fourth asks disturbing questions.

Thinking about these tendencies, I came up with a few examples of how they seem to work in adult literature:

1. *Reshaping the world* through instantly memorable characters who start popping up in real life once you've read about them. So the novel pinpoints patterns in social behaviour that the reader might miss — and as a result these patterns become inscribed in real life. A book is a template.

2. *Documentary-style* descriptions of societies where the place shapes the story. So each location has characteristics that resemble a human personality. In fact I believe that all settings in books imply a living subject behind them — an animal, person or god — otherwise they tend to lack interest.

3. *The mind's eye view*, like poetry, can rearrange the ordinary laws of language and alter psychological perception. I call this the Van Gogh approach.

4. *The questioning approach* which uses ambiguity and multi-layered meaning to frame moments of heightened importance. So the writer aims, unlike the lawyer, at words that carry more than one meaning, contradictory feelings and moral dilemmas. Complexity through truth to life.

In some ways these four examples resemble what John Ruskin called the *pathetic fallacy*,[1] they ascribe feelings to the surrounding world. But Ruskin was attacking the artificial personification of nature in 18th century writing, whereas I'm thinking of the deliberate foregrounding of subjective, expressive experience in modern writing and art — a technique used by Turner in his painting of the *Ariel in a snowstorm*, and vigorously defended by Ruskin against its Victorian critics.

As a young reader I lived my books. I didn't think much about them, I

---

[1] Ruskin, John (1856). Of the Pathetic Fallacy. Modern Painters, volume iii. pt. 4.

simply picked up the next one and read it. This seems to point to a fifth principle: the integration of all these tendencies into a holistic experience. What I call *flow*, a one-way movement like the arrow of time, where digressions and reversals are possible as long as the psychological line holds. That, to me, is the essence of an exciting book.

# STORIES LEAD TO STORIES

Thirty years ago, when I taught in London, I came across a short story called *Bud's Luck*. It was about a quiet, dreamy schoolboy who finds a magic coin that keeps coming back to him. He uses it to clear all the local slot machines of sweets and chewing gum, stockpiling more than he can ever eat. But when Bud shares his 'winnings' with his classmates, his luck becomes a curse. Word gets around that Bud has been spotted emptying machines and every evening a different gang shows up to bully him and steal the coin. The next day he's beaten up again because the coin disappeared into the machine and didn't work. And when the boys find the magic coin resting snuggly in Bud's pocket, it sets off another beating.

In desperation Bud drops the coin down a drain, leaves it on a railway line and flings it in a river, but every morning the coin returns and he has to set off, alone but quietly resigned, to face school and his angry classmates ...

After reading *Bud's Luck* I discovered a much earlier version called *Abu Kasem's Slippers*. The original Iraqi story goes like this:

A wealthy merchant named Abu Kasem was famous in Baghdad for his miserliness, his ability to drive a hard bargain, and his slippers — which were old, worn, patched, and stained. One day, after forcing a bankrupt to sell off some fine rose oil and beautiful crystal bottles, Abu went to the public baths to celebrate his winnings. In there he met a friend, a fellow-merchant, who insisted he must buy some new slippers. "I've been thinking about this myself," Abu said, "but I do believe they have a few more miles in them," and he went in to enjoy his bath. While he was inside the Chief Judge of Baghdad came to take a bath. Abu finished first. When he returned to the dressing room he found, to his surprise, that his slippers had disappeared and a lovely new pair had taken their place. "Well," Abu thought to himself, "my friend must have decided to honour me with a gift. Maybe he thinks it good business to win the favour of a rich man like me." So Abu put on the beautiful new slippers and went home. When the judge emerged from the bath and discovered Abu's disgusting, tattered slippers in place of his own, he immediately sent for the culprit. Abu spent a night in jail and paid a very heavy fine. The next day an angry Abu threw his old slippers out of the window. But they fell into a fisherman's net who threw them straight back — right into the middle of Abu's table, breaking the perfume bottles and spilling the oil ...

For the rest of the story Abu tries every possible way to rid himself of the slippers: burying them, driving them out of town and dropping them in a pond, even burning them. But the slippers keep returning, creating havoc along the way. Finally, back in court for injuring an elderly peasant woman while throwing away the slippers, Abu pleads with the judge to stop holding him responsible for the actions of his old slippers.

The judge frees Abu on condition that he takes the peasant woman and her husband into his house. It is only then that Abu is finally able to discard the slippers in the rubbish bin and never see them again.

And the interpretation?

From a Jungian perspective, Bud and Abu are both obsessives. They cut themselves off, returning constantly to the same enclosed space where they can experience the highs and lows of addiction. And in that condition the fetishized object replaces who they are. It becomes their badge, a stand-in self that intervenes between them and direct experience. They are trapped in Maya, the world of illusion, narrowing everything to a defensive formulation. In the end what they have to do is free themselves from the enchantment of objects, give up their self-absorption and accept a smaller role in life.

*Bud's Luck* and *Abu Kaseem's Slippers* connect for me with *the Ghost of Christmas Past* and the book of *Job*. They're narratives of hubris, suffering, and partial redemption. They also suggested an idea which my wife Sue Hampton used in her book *Frank*. In Sue's children's story the little Splat monster becomes so annoying that Frank has to get rid of it. But every time he tries to destroy or abandon Splat the red dough monster returns, of course.

And the moral — if there is one?

Stories lead to stories and take part of their power from that tradition, but as with anything living, there are always individual variations shaping what's passed on.

# NOT THE DEATH OF THE AUTHOR

*Skyscrapers are not raised simply to conceal dead mice*
— Saul Bellow

I find that the best writing comes out of the dark. Often it starts from a single word, a thought or an incident that sets off a search — which I'm experiencing now, writing this piece — involving lots of stops and false starts.

While I'm searching I try out phrases and listen to how the words sound, judging their effect on the reader. I'm also editing every sentence as I go, juggling the phrases to achieve the most elegant formulation and removing words that overburden it. At the same time I'm plugging gaps, enhancing effects and reading back to ensure continuity. In addition, and crucially, I'm writing for feel, mood and flow, visualising the incidents and riding the emotional waves as I go.

I draw on long-term schemas when I'm writing. So I've thought through my most important life experiences, tracing their patterns and bundling them into meaningful wholes. Usually it's the painful moments that count — the confusions of youth, the breakdown of relationships and hidden dreams and losses. But the writing mustn't be too pumped-up. The feelings may spark but the heat they generate has to be contained. In fact when I reach a climax I don't experience it directly, I just watch it develop. I think of this phase as *cold fire*. It's a dream move, rather like the runner's experience when the body takes over. It's been described in various fields of activity as being 'wired in', 'in the zone' or 'playing the A-game'. And the more skill you have, through keeping in practice and setting the right goals, the easier the flow ...

That's when writing comes easiest, but it has to be steered or ridden as it goes its own way. Shaping is all. There isn't a route one and it can't be reduced to a formula. Most of all, it takes skill, care over details and repeated attempts. As Saul Bellow said about the novel: 'Skyscrapers are not raised simply to conceal dead mice.' So it's not quick, it's not therapy and it isn't a trick.

Saul Bellow's remark has that doubleness of meaning which characterises great quotes. He could be rejecting the Freudian theory of art as a defence mechanism against neurosis or he could be criticising whodunits. Both see art as a concealment process. So the reader's job is to break the code, guess the hidden secret and 'explain' the story. It's like trying out a bunch of keys in a door knowing there's only one that fits. Sometimes there are a number of possible readings, but it's still rather different to open-ended fiction. In this kind of book it's important to give nothing away and avoid too much elaboration. Paradoxically, this flat, stripped-down style, with its clever, impersonal effects invites the reader to see through to the artificial nature of the writing. Some post-modern thinkers praise this approach which allows, they say, a 'democratic' space where the reader is at the centre of the action, trying to guess *Quo Vadis?* or *What Would You Do If This Happened To You?* Often these plot-twists have a 'gaming' aspect to them, relying heavily on shock tactics drawn from mixed conventions and genres. So everything is in flux and the author simply shuffles the cards. It's clever, value-free and against 'closure'. Most of all, it claims to deconstruct elitist culture − though the theories of postmodernism are expressed in a rarefied code exclusive to those in the know.

What postmoderns call 'transparency' can be an excuse to write conventional stories that manipulate ideas but fail to create rounded characters. The result, in some cases, is thin writing where the sketch is valued above the finished work and minor characters take over the role of protagonists. As Kurt Vonnegut said: 'Give your readers as much information as possible as soon as possible. To hell with suspense. Readers should have such a complete understanding of what is going on, where and why, that they could finish the story themselves, should cockroaches eat the last few pages.'

Another take on writing is the jigsaw metaphor. In this the writer shifts around chunks of story, or strips of language, fitting them together according to traditional patterns. It's rather Platonic and beautiful, often minimalist, and moves us in familiar ways. Sometimes called 'classic', it assumes that there is a correct formulation the writer is trying to find. For me, this is a traditional route that gives direction but can also present false trails and walled-in gardens where the real and current life never gets a look-in. Its pleasing symmetry can divert from the real task, which is to peer into the unknown.

Writing, for me, is like wriggling into a hiding place through a narrow entrance. It reminds me of entering the hollowed-out space I discovered beneath the hedge as a child. There I could watch the world through a leaf screen, filtering experience while looking out for new developments. Although it felt special in my own secret hideout, I was also alone and rather cut off. The hedge was a raw, spiky barrier but also a peephole, transforming perception so everything was seen from 'the other side'.

Writing is unpredictable. The flow of language isn't always there. At times it's a radio in the head, a fitful collection of words and half-tunes that stop and start and come and go like the sound of a distant event carried on the breeze. Sometimes it's close-up and insistent but at other times it pulls away, becoming garbled and clichéd. And it's in need of constant adjustment as it drifts off the station, becoming muddy or confused.

There are other metaphors, too. Writing can be a show garden where the styles run together in a carefully-planted mixture of formal and wild. Or it can be an archaeological dig where the finds are fitted together imaginatively to conjure up another time and place.

More prosaically, writing can be a sorting exercise, combining Cinderella's task of separating the good and bad lentils with a game of Pairs. So when I find that a subject brings with it a whole, fully-formed vocabulary, I write the words down in lists and keep trying out different combinations, hoping to find a fit. When I'm full of phrases like this I see it as a good sign and believe that I'll complete my daily word quota without too much effort. Unfortunately, a mechanical approach usually leads to a dead end where it's *never quite there.* So by the end of the day I find myself unsuccessfully repeating phrases I've tried and rejected to see if I've 'heard them right'.

It's this sounding out process against the inner ear that ultimately decides the flow of a written piece. Words fit together or they don't according to their music, and the detailed edit that attempts to adjust them to a clear logical order and 'reader-friendly' format has to be just that — a secondary elaboration. Sound is sense is story. To settle for less is to ignore the voice in the ear, warning against safe, well-crafted, middle-of-the-road writing that aims to do no more than put on a game show for passing entertainment. I prefer the writing that allows for ambiguity and character development, which isn't contained within a style box, where the meaning develops from imagery and register, and the words shine a light into the contradictions of the human heart.

At the end of writing this piece I have a long tail of unused sentences. They are the background voices that didn't quite make it but add in colour, light and shade. Without them I couldn't have written anything.

# MY IMAGINARY AUTOBIOGRAPHY

*And the task of writing is to hang on tight, like Menelaus, till the god gives up, stops trying to throw his rider, and becomes his true self.*

In my imaginary autobiography I'm sneaking between fences along an overgrown passageway dividing Fifties suburban back gardens. I'm shaky inside as I step around orange fungi and fat-bodied spiders while poking sticks into webs. Part of me is watchful, an undercover agent observing neighbours through gaps in the fence, and part of me is hot and sweaty, sniffing out a trail.

In another scene I'm by the house with an old wooden chair that I've been told to break up. It's my chance to let it have it, full force. The chair's in my power, so I twist and wrench it, exercising my will. There's a beast inside me, a smasher and basher who does what he likes and enjoys what he can do.

At other times in the story I'm a ghost and I walk through walls. This allows me to live in unseen worlds, overhearing chatter in houses and listening in to children talking in playgrounds. I can tune in to friends as they speak and be there with the neighbours at any time of day. I can even enter the heads of strangers, living their lives as an unseen watcher ...

For years I was planning my imaginary autobiography. I wanted to find words for the baroque and the surreal hidden inside suburban living, the prisoner at the window, the digger of tunnels and the boy who could soar and turn cartwheels over roofs. But my crazy memories didn't transfer well to paper. They were states of being rather than anecdotes, they didn't build or develop, and they were too absurd to appear in a conventional autobiography. I needed entertaining incidents that went somewhere and what I had was a collection of static tableaux.

I think of them now as defences. As an only child I was a lonely, over-protected boy who lacked confidence. There was a space around me, an absence of love or relatedness, and the fantasies were an outlet for my pent-up feelings. I was also sneaky. I thought people would laugh if they read about my 'real' thoughts and I wanted to avoid the critical parental eye. So I made my words tediously elaborate, straining for effect, or crafted low-key indirect 'poetic' versions of MY LIFE — but neither rang true. It's hard to write about essence or deep subjectivity and, linguistically, the subject I'd chosen was as impossibly silly as my dreams of walking tightropes or scaling cliffs.

What I also didn't realise was how much editing any written piece requires and how an esoteric subject demands even more work.

If it was ever going to exist, my imaginary autobiography would begin by describing the Odyssean journey of a pink-faced child being wheeled in a pram down a N. London street. The houses are islands and the street's a sea, turning into ocean when we reach the shops. Feeling the wind striking through flesh, the child becomes a schoolboy running, deer-like across open fields, transforming to a fox jumping a ditch. There are flames close behind, licking at his back. The boy, or animal, reaches sand and a long, curving, seascape where he walks with his father exploring continents and changing, as the sun goes down, into a seal playing in water ...

The film cuts suddenly to a suburban bedroom where I'm lying awake in bed making seal-like noises. *Awru, awru* I bark, flapping my hands, till my father bursts in, ordering me to sleep. At that point the waves rise up and the film ends. Next morning I'm absent, flown in spirit from my body, while the person I imitate eats breakfast, gets washed and dressed and walks out into the garden to hide behind fences.

Looking back at that child and at what I've written, I think the presiding spirit of my imaginary autobiography is Proteus, the sea god, who changes into something different every time his questioner tries to grasp him. These shape-changing transformations, which Pessoa called heteronymity,[1] resemble the masks of Comedy and Tragedy at a Greek drama. And the task of writing is to hang on tight, like Menelaus,[2] till the god gives up, stops trying to throw his rider, and becomes his true self.

These words are the result.

----

1 'For each of his "voices", Pessoa conceived a highly distinctive poetic idiom and technique, a complex biography, a context of literary influence and polemics and, most arrestingly of all, subtle interrelations and reciprocities of awareness.' George Steiner, "A man of many parts", in The Observer, Sunday, 3 June 2001.

2 According to Homer (Odyssey iv:412), Menelaus, who was becalmed on Pharos on his journey home from the Trojan War, learned that if he could capture Proteus, he could force him to reveal which of the gods he had offended and how he could return home. Proteus emerged from the sea to sleep among his colony of seals, but Menelaus was successful in holding him, though Proteus took the forms of a lion, a serpent, a leopard, a pig, even of water or a tree. Proteus then became himself, answering Menelaus's questions truthfully.

# GETTING THE GIST OF IT

According to the Fuzzy-Trace Theory,[1] our brains use two cognitive methods: *gist* and *verbatim*.

♪  *Gist* thinking is intuitive and springs from general feel.

♪  *Verbatim* thinking is exact and relies on detailed representations.

When we take decisions we often use *gist* – going by rough approximations based on previous experience – even though *verbatim* is more reliably analytic.

The Fuzzy-Trace Theory also suggests that children who give witness without adult 'guidance' tell it *verbatim*, as it is. Adults on the other hand often rely on *gist*, giving false 'secondary elaborations'. Their memories are patchy or bundled up into 'feeling schemas' based on information picked up after the event. So adults are unreliable narrators, turning small hints and suggestions into full-blown scenarios which never really happened. Or to put it another way: believe Maisie, not the butler.

The piece below is about childhood. It's also about memory. Given that words have precise meanings and that *things* bring a scene to life, I worked on it as an accurately detailed, *verbatim* representation ...

*** 

'When I was a child there were certain qualities that seemed to be locked into experience. One was pain, or fear of pain. I can still feel the raw jolting shock of trapping my fingers in the car door. It happened without warning like touching a hot electric fire and I was crying, then it went numb, leaving a gut memory. Equally visceral in a different way was the moment in our quiet back garden when a woman jumped up from her chair and began screaming. I found out afterwards that she'd been stung by a wasp.

Later on I became familiar with the weary, uphill pain of cross-country running: the stitch in the side, the breathlessness and the heavy, swollen legs, turning to water afterwards. It was surprising how pain could take over the whole body, concentrating everything to a single point or hollow-

1 Reyna, V.F. & Brainerd, C.J. (1995). Fuzzy-trace theory: An interim synthesis. Learning and Individual Differences. 7: 1–75.

ing out flesh to nothing.

Surprise was another, related, childhood experience. Words didn't connect or lost their meanings, people would appear through doors like actors and things would happen without warning. At school I listened but struggled with meaning. So my reactions in P.E. were slow and muddled like an out-of-synch film, and when shown how to jump or land or shin up a rope I was left standing when the others had finished. Nothing seemed to register. It was as if I was being lectured in an unfamiliar language at the other end of a long-distance phone call. In class questions were asked and knowledge was tested at odd times, using strange codes and yes-no answers, while orders and corrections seemed to appear like fiats from above. There was a mysterious presumption of guilt in much of this, rather like Kafka's *Trial.*

Christmas and birthdays were full of surprise of a different kind. Anticipation-surprise made everything pleasurably breathless and charged with significance, like the moment in a theatre when the lights dim and the curtain goes up. Rooms and objects glowed, faces smiled and anything could happen.

Fascination, together with strangeness, was built in to childhood. I pretended that the wallpaper in my bedroom was a strange land, part-jungle, part-dream, that the curtains were maps and the carpet was a featureless grassland where I went in search of food with my own small band of hunter-gatherers. In the garden I stepped arms-out over the stones in the path, avoiding the cracks, as if I was fording a river. And I had my own secret ritualised acts: right foot first putting on shoes, left-hand-only holding a cup, and climbing to the bathroom two stairs at a time.

The strange encounters of childhood included the staked-up broad beans lengthening slowly at the bottom of the garden, clothes pegs and scrubbing brushes hidden beneath the sink, hairline cracks in plaster above my bed and Jack Frost growths on the inside of windows.

I remember my childhood as strange, sometimes painful and often surprising. These were my fixed stars and I was in the middle, living in the moment, with everything around me, while watching from the outside as if my experience was invented, a version of events I'd just made up.'

$$***$$

Reading back my piece afterwards I realised that I'd focused on moods and feelings; so the writing described states of *being*, rather than actions. The solid, tangible surface was there but, like Impressionism, at strange angles and in close-up, exposing the patterns underneath. It wasn't cinema vérité but it captured my feelings.

In terms of the Fuzzy-Trace Theory, it was more broad-brush, more *gist* than *verbatim*, but to get there I'd used detail. And my written-out memories, now I had them on the page, seemed more real, more actual and truly substantial, than anything first-hand or factual that might or might not have happened ...

# MEMORY

*The child is father to the man*
— Wordsworth


I remember our first house: a pebble-dashed semi-D in Colindale, North London. It seemed tall, like Bluebeard's Castle, with high concrete front steps as if it was raised on a rock and had to be scaled by hauling yourself up with a rope and a ladder. Inside was dark — or it seems dark now, looking inside — and large, like a cave, though cleaner of course. The house had a silent, neutral quality like a retreat but also a practical, active busyness as my mother cleaned and cooked while I looked on and sometimes helped her. It's a present-tense house even though it's from the Fifties, a house of the mind where nothing ever changes, like heaven or a museum, but at the same time it's an all-go place full of action and drama and stereoscopic vision.

So I see myself on washing days standing on a chair in front of the sink, plunging the clothes into soapy water, and simultaneously sitting on the far side of the room with pools on lino, steam in the air and my red-faced mother telling me to sit still. As my vision moves, camera-like into the back room, I see her crouched forward at the sewing machine, stitching cloth with one foot pumping the treadle — but what attracts my attention and leads me to another, much quieter memory is a collection of strange-shaped metal attachments in the side drawer. Pulling out one, I finger it — something I'm not allowed to do — and trace its thin silver shape, which is a cross between a dentist's brace and a cheese-cutter.

The memories are contradictory. So I'm crawling under the dining table, playing at being an animal in a den, while sitting, straight-backed at the table eating my supper. I'm in a pram parked in the garden while standing on the path gazing, amazed, at washing dancing on the line. Later, or earlier, I'm in the back room pretending to read while rolling Plasticine into a ball which at some point I shall lob through the steamed-up French windows. Then, upstairs, I morph into a nice, well-behaved, domesticated child helping my mother tuck in blankets while simultaneously bouncing on the mattress to block her bed-making.

Attention-seeking and private, my memories want it both ways. They run wild and shout, clowning on the beach, and freeze behind walls dodging the missiles at school; they're an album full of smiley, waving family and imaginary battles where the boy-hero turns tail; they're sacrificial and they're deceitful, sober or fantastical and can't be challenged or verified – yet their truth is undeniable.

Looking back, I often wonder about the accuracy and authenticity of my memories. I believe that some of the pictures I see are fictions built up from things said about my childhood. I'm also aware that memories cluster around strong feelings and that passion can simplify an incident, making it more cut-and-dried, like evidence in court. But with hindsight I've come to see my past as a range of possibilities where doubt and certainty mix. And that idea has helped me to piece together an 'alternative history' of my childhood. It's about selection, adjustment and retrospective analysis. So my idea of what happened changes as I make allowances for the Fifties – an era full of remarks such as 'praise makes a child big-headed' and 'a good beating never did me any harm'.

I have a vivid, tactile memory of being beaten, in my case with a rubber tube. The stinging, curled-up violence sets off earlier memories of being hit by snowballs or watching two boys fighting, one knocking the other's head against brickwork and drawing blood. Pain and fear foreshorten these memories, like an imaginary car journey that misses out the business of getting there and sees only the crash at the end.

Compared with those school memories my time at home feels softer and more protected, both familiar and strange, allowing for magic and multiple possibilities. It's a place I go back to when I write, using what's called Guided Imagery or Creative Visualisation[1] with its four main techniques:

1. Image generation.
2. Image maintenance.
3. Image inspection.
4. Image transformation.

I've used all four techniques in writing this piece, with the aim of turning

---

1 'Creative visualization is the cognitive process of purposefully generating visual mental imagery, with eyes open or closed, simulating or recreating visual perception, in order to maintain, inspect, and transform those images, consequently modifying their associated emotions or feelings, with intent to experience a subsequent beneficial physiological, psychological, or social effect, such as expediting the healing of wounds to the body, minimizing physical pain, alleviating psychological pain including anxiety, sadness, and low mood, improving self-esteem or self-confidence, and enhancing the capacity to cope when interacting with others.' Wikipedia.

so-called 'fact' into a creative act based on what seems likely. Like a scientific theory it's what the evidence points towards. My past is in there, all the more true for appearing in several different versions.

Or to put it another way, our memories are a best-guess scenario guided by:
♪   feelings
♪   random remarks
♪   retrospective elaborations
and the work we put into them.

# FEELING FOR THE PAST

The *von Restorff effect*[1] says that when several similar ideas are presented, the one that differs from the rest is more likely to be remembered. So my memory of seaside holidays could be summed up by the list:
sea
waves
rocks
apron strings
wind
bare sand.

The apron strings were my granny's. Egged on by my grandpa, I knotted them from behind when she was busy at the sink. Her outrage when she realised what I'd done was all part of the game. "By, I'll tan that lad!" she shouted in panto-style as she struggled with the strings. I can still see her now, red-faced and flustered, waving her fist from the kitchen. She acted up, but didn't really see the joke.

I remember the apron strings story because suddenly being naughty was allowed. There were rules at home and strict routines, but holidays were different. With my grandpa I could clown and show off; it was a case of big dog, little dog; if he could play practical jokes then so could I.

He dared me to lock my gran in the pantry, bribing me with sweets. When I did she banged on the door as if there was a fire. It was my job to release her — and exit the kitchen at a run. One of my pranks, suggested by him, was hiding her glasses. I also had the task of shooing flies or pretending there was someone at the door while he conducted his raids on the sugar bowl.

My grandpa was a wag. The stories he told were whoppers about people he'd met and medals he'd won. He was a short man with foxy eyes and a permanent grin who collected playing cards and Andy Cap cartoons. At

1 Parker, Amanda; Wilding, Edward & Akerman, Colin (1998). The von Restorff Effect in Visual Object Recognition Memory in Humans and Monkeys: The Role of Frontal/Perirhinal Interaction. Journal of Cognitive Neuroscience. 10 (6): 691–703.

home he was the 'lad', in public he was the man with the silver-plated stopwatch and the trilby. And in his relationship with his wife he used me as his fall guy.

It's the contrast to the uniform background that makes the unusual memory stand out. So visiting my grandparents was like entering a reconstruction of a pre-war house. It was two up, two down with a back extension, crowded with furniture and full of ticking and chiming clocks. The shelves in the back room held old atlases and local history books, Toby Jugs lined the mantelpiece, and the pantry smelled of vinegar and spices. It was homely and old-fashioned — not the sort of place where you'd expect to find conflict. But looking back, I realise that my grandpa's teasing had a hidden underside — which is why, perhaps, I remember it.

My granny's hands shook so badly that she'd clatter the cups when serving guests. The saucers ended up awash with tea. At the time I was told she suffered from nerves. I remember her sitting, short of breath, and hearing the word angina. I realise now that the teasing and joking amounted to bullying.

The apron strings and my grandmother's hands stand out because they seem to fit the era. In theory they might seem unusual — and therefore memorable — but their real significance is emotional. What brings them to mind is the ever-present sense I had of being watched over, taken to task at school and at home, and told what to do. Bossiness and disapproval were widespread in the Fifties, so kicking over the traces with my grandpa seemed exciting, and the person we made fun off was one of the bossiest. I remember how she told me to speak like a man, stand up straight and grow up to be a soldier. She knew what was 'best for me', fussing over proper clothes and haircuts, so my childish reaction was to 'do the other', taking pleasure in breaking taboos — though of course the tricks I played on her were cruel, unnecessary and dangerous.

In the *Stanislavski System* 'affective memory' is the process of recalling feelings from an event in the past and 'playing them out' in a current scenario. Taught by Lee Strasberg and called *The Method*, it involved, in the words of Elia Kazan: 'recalling the circumstances, physical and personal, surrounding an intensely emotional experience in the actor's past'. Elia goes on: 'Lee taught his actors to launch their work on every scene by taking a minute to remember the details surrounding the emotional experience in their lives that would correspond to the emotion of the scene they were about to play. "Take a minute!" became the watchword ...'

Taking a minute for my childhood returns me to that house. I've a picture in my head of stone hot water bottles, ice on the windowpanes and Davenport plates. The feelings guide me as I enter the front door with an imaginary camera. The hallway is dark but I can see the wooden coat stand at the bottom of the stairs. I'm following my memories into the crowded back room with my grandpa filling in his pools by the fire and my granny baking in the stone-floored kitchen. They can't see me as I explore the cupboards, downstairs and upstairs, pulling out jigsaws and Christmas decorations. I'm turning the pages of my grandpa's stamp album while drinking Tizer and eating my gran's cheese straws — and I'm a child in a house playing out my feelings, dark and light, as I remember the detail of

apron strings
door locks
sugar bowls
my granny's shaking hands
Toby Jugs
saucers
clocks

and me now writing, re-creating memory, imagining my story.

# THE TIME OF TRIAL

*This is a man's, man's, man's, man's world but it wouldn't be nothing, nothing without a woman*
— James Brown

I was nine when the bullying began. I remember walking home from school followed by a gang of small boys. They hunted in a pack, laughing and shouting out names from a distance. Every afternoon I shut out their calls and kept going in the hope they'd get tired and try someone else. As I walked I told myself I wasn't really there. Part of me felt that *they* had the upper hand — so if I fought and lost that would be shameful but if I beat them up then I'd be the bully. I was afraid that if I turned around they'd see my tears and call out even more and if I tried to catch them they'd dodge like flies, jeering at my clumsiness. And like those flies, they were dirty and demanding, and there was nothing I could do to shake them off.

So why did it happen?

At school I wanted to sit with the girls. They were clever and they listened; they were nicer, kinder and had quick hands and pretty hair. In the playground they ran fast, linked arms and called out strange words or mysterious numbers as they practised skipping or hopscotch. Everything about them seemed cleaner, more intelligently respectful and civilised. And if a boy challenged them they didn't have to fight.

The boys soon found my weak spots. If they challenged or insulted me I was slow to catch on. There was a time delay while I tried to find an answer and my reply, when it came, wasn't that clever. I gave myself away, blushing at rude things or pretending not to hear when one of them burped or swore. In me they recognised a quick, easy, guaranteed laugh and they enjoyed seeing how far they could push me.

I remember swimming lessons. Stripped down to my trunks and paraded with my classmates along the edge of a blue and white pool, I felt cold, exposed and inadequate. The swimming baths were large and echoey with nowhere to hide. Everyone could see me as I struggled alone and helpless at the shallow end pretending to swim while clinging onto my red rubber ring. Later, when I moved out to deeper water, I tried to please, bobbing up and down and calling excitedly. It was when our instructor told me to strike out and swim that I floundered, my mouth filled up, and I went under. Each week I was told loudly to SWIM and each week I struggled to the poolside, spluttering and thrashing in a parody of drowning. And every time I lost my nerve, my next attempt was blocked by my own fear of failure.

At ten I moved from London to Sheffield, where the bullying became more physical. Although I was tall for my age, some of the boys at my new school were taller and stronger than me. I was the outsider, and this time, instead of shouting from a distance, one of them decided to call me out in the playground. In the fight that followed he floored me in front of his admiring followers and punch-wrestled me to submission. I was anybody's after that, the girl-boy who everyone took on and insulted, because kids with a 'rep' knew I wouldn't answer back.

It was the silence inside me that gave them their power. I'd a sense of being watched and judged, I was no good at sport — a dodger at the back who couldn't catch a ball — and I took myself ultra-seriously, but what made me a victim was my own shocked silence. I'd no self-possession, nothing to fall back on. I'd no snappy-catch answers and, as in sport, I couldn't connect or act without thinking.

We moved again, this time to Northumberland and a boys' grammar school where I was singled out by P. He was the class hard man: a dark, hairy youth with a powerful jaw and penetrating eyes which he fixed on me like a boxer. He probed me with rude, gloating personal questions. I answered him back once and he challenged me to an after-school fight, which I at first accepted but then lost my nerve and sneaked off home. From then on, he insulted me at will, elbowing me to one side in queues and jabbing me with pens and scissors, calling me his worm. I didn't dare say a word. His status rose as he reduced mine to nothing, and though I believe the teachers knew or at least suspected, they turned a blind eye.

What I experienced with P was the school of hard knocks where team sport was the measure of success and the staff were either indifferent or violent, using nicknames and beatings and slaps around the head. P was the outcome of their methods. As long as they could keep him in line then everyone else would kowtow.

What no one offered was a set of male values that mirrored what I'd seen amongst the girls. They smiled and held hands, enjoyed talk and fine motor skills and were physical in a way I admired and saw as self-possessed. Thinking of boys as boasters and fighters, and therefore lacking, I imagined girls to be deeper and more mature, or at least more experienced and wiser to the world.

I'd been measured and found wanting in a man's world that kept me quiet. As Robert W. Fuller says the boys were *rankists*,[1] claiming special privileges, standing on the shoulders of others. But in the end, and maybe as a result of the bullying, I came to see that all boys are afraid and that fear shuts them up. What they and I needed was a different set of values, an open, authentic exchange between equals, talking about strengths and weaknesses and acknowledging feelings in a world that was nothing without the girls.

1 Fuller, Robert W. (2003) Somebodies and Nobodies: Overcoming the Abuse of Rank. Gabriola Island, Canada: New Society Publishers. ISBN 0-86571-486-X.

# WRESTLING WITH MY ANGEL

I grew up wanting to be a spiritual child. I didn't see grand visions or hear strange voices and my world was small, measured by school times and mealtimes and trips to see the family. But in private spots and in places I visited there was a pictorial quality, a sense of something extra, an additional factor that filtered in, making for significance. It was visible but elusive, an edge to experience unnoticed by anyone else, like a signal from a distance that doesn't transmit and yet somehow registers. I was witness to impressions that couldn't be named.

But being spiritual didn't come easily. Religious Education was boring and closing your eyes in school assemblies was considered a sign of weakness, so the head-down lads would pull monkey faces and wink at each other. They teased boys like me as odd or airy-fairy. Given their persistence and the widespread adult reluctance to discuss 'personal matters' it was surprising that I held onto my spirituality at all. My parents thought of themselves as reasonable, down-to-earth people who viewed prayers as slightly suspect and congregations as stand-offish, so going to church was Christmas-time-only. I think the war had interrupted regular worship, there was a reaction against rationing or 'making-do', and as belief waned, people wanted gadgets not God.

My spirituality was untutored, expressing itself in vague longings in parks and gardens and a love of music. I found patterns in brick, secret messages in worm casts and ant runs, and moments of immersion in the change of seasons. On holiday, the wind on the seafront moved me while the view out to sea filled me with breathless excitement. And to keep up my high I began, as I got older, to take myself off on long country walks quoting poetry in my head — and sometimes out loud — searching for uplift. The hypnotic rhythm of my steps filled my thoughts as I worked at being spiritual, driving my feelings to be wild and strange and mystically inspired. I fed my moods, imitating Richard Jeffries in *The Story of my Heart* with his cultivated intensity and longing for 'soul-life'. Still later, I came to see myself as a mediaeval mystic, cut off from life, experiencing visions similar to the Temptation of St Anthony, feeling haunted and hunted and spiritually exposed. I wanted to be a poet so I looked for signs — the exact angle of a broken fence, a skyline, a flower, stones in water —

and I made myself sensitive, directing my attention to memorising every detail with a straining, urgent need for elevation. I wrestled alone with my angel. And yet, nothing seemed to change. I wasn't saved or inspired or lifted out of myself. I remained time-limited and vulnerable. And the poetry I wrote was embarrassing.

The obvious conclusion was that my spirituality had to be forced because it wasn't authentic. In a sense I was trying to bully myself — or, as my parents might have said, 'getting above myself' — straining to realise 'the other' as a concrete, graspable, here-and-now experience. I'd not understood metaphor or symbol and still believed a spade was a spade was a spade. As a result my faith was attempting to move mountains. In any case, from a Buddhist perspective, my longing for 'spiritual experience' introduced a false split between 'experiencer' and 'experienced'. Rather than simply being, I was trapped within false opposites.

At the same time, the youth I was becoming pooh-poohed it all. I had another, rather sneery voice telling my spiritual child to be quiet, that the film he was running in his head was a projection of his own fear and self-importance — a view I embraced later when I read Freud's ideas on religion. I came to see my spiritual boy as a neurotic illusionist trying to boost himself with a few cheap tricks. He was in the grip of superstition and his need for a sign was a child asking for the impossible.

But putting the spiritual behind me left a gap. I tried to fill it with Marxism but the behaviour of its followers put me off. Later I adopted Existentialism's notion of conditional belief as a deliberate choice, but it left me feeling empty. Without warmth or transport life was flat. It was better to strain and be pumped-up than to walk away — and the path I was avoiding was the hard slog back to the crazy poetry-boy and his fight with the angel.

So the romantic but self-aware believer is still part of me. His transports are mine, now realised in the certainty of doubt, the via negativa[1] and the silence. I don't need miracles, just deepened understanding. And it's in remembering my absurd flights of fancy as the spiritual child — that wide-eyed, speculative and contradictory state of being where the world is charged with something additional — that I now find God.

---

1 'The via negativa is a type of theological thinking that attempts to describe God, the Divine Good, by negation, to speak only in terms of what may not be said about the perfect goodness that is God.' — Nicholas Bunnin and Jiyuan Yu: *Negative Theology: The Blackwell Dictionary of Western Philosophy.*

'We do not know what God is. God Himself does not know what He is because He is not anything. Literally God is not, because He transcends being.' — John Scotus Erigena.

*Novels testify and they adapt life. They're a gift, like a child, not a commodity, and they grow up slowly.*

*Life can be messy and repetitious, books are composed.*

*To be expert in any expressive art form you mustn't fool yourself that something is good enough. It can always be better.*

# 6th MOVEMENT

## CONDITIONS OF THE HEART

### What readers said about:
*The Way of Illness*

Virginia Woolf, in writing on illness, described how much it could make us aware of the world. Leslie Tate deftly, carefully, courageously, adds to Woolf by reminding us of the necessity of empathy, of compassion. As a former athlete who also suffers from disintegrating discs, as a poet who has learned from that pain a language of hope, I am moved by Leslie Tate's thoughtful and precise memoir. And grateful.
— *Mark Statman, International Poet, Translator and former Associate Professor of Literary Studies at Eugene Lang College NYC.*

Innovative and wise, *Heaven's Rage* reinvents a language for pain and reminds us of life's many surprising pleasures.
— *Emma Claire Sweeney, Novelist longlisted for the Not The Booker Prize.*

The writer's job is to present us not only with beauty and distractions, but with the harsh realities of our lives, the parts we don't usually discuss. Leslie Tate writes honestly, from a place lacking pretension, about pain and the different ways that we deal with it. It is a privilege to be let into such a space of vulnerability. This is a side of being human we should all read about before we need to (inevitably) face pain.
—*Miriam Calleja, Author of Pomegranate Heart, Poems in Maltese and English.*

This piece achieves true alchemy! By moving back and forth between his own and others' illnesses, Leslie Tate shows us the mirror-like nature of identity. So we become ourselves through relationships, through the mirroring we experience in our encounters with others. Often, that connection comes through suffering — when we may not act our 'best', but we can become the best of the possible selves we can be. This 'best' self naturally extends compassion to others in their time of need. This new self is also more creative than before, for to be creative is to invent — and necessity is the mother of invention. So if we learn to cope with illness and remain whole, we emerge with greater resources. Then we can do more with less, creating something from less than nothing, and transforming ugliness into beauty. This is how alchemy is accomplished.

— *Joe Rhinewine, Psychotherapist and Musician.*

In poetry and prose, Leslie Tate takes us through the horror and helplessness of battling with your body, ending with remarkable insights about how to face a changed life with courage and hope.

— *Nayna Kumari, Body Psychotherapist and Counsellor, BA(Hons), PGCE, RSA (Dip), MA, MAR, MBACP.*

Drawing on his own illness experience of himself and two resilient friends, Leslie Tate explores the psychological and physical effects of pain and how different people deal with it.

— *Judith Perera, Journalist/Editor.*

# THE WAY OF ILLNESS

*It is easier to find men who will volunteer to die, than to find
those who are willing to endure pain with patience*
— Julius Caesar

*One small crack does not mean that you are broken; it means
that you were put to the test and you didn't fall apart*
— Linda Poindexter

Physical pain has its limits — or so I believed until one morning, dressing
for work, I felt something give in my back. It was sudden and sharp, like
a stick breaking. Soon my whole lumbar region was burning.

Forcing myself downstairs, I rubbed in muscle balm and drove to work.
But as the hot electric jolts intensified, I pulled up. No amount of crying
out or squeezing the steering wheel could get me through. The pain was
bigger than I was. Turning the car around I drove back to my flat, phoned
work and went to bed with hot water bottles and painkillers.

I'd had back problems before. As a child I lived with niggling aches and
occasional stabbing pains. They came and went but when, during one
attack, I began to limp, my parents intervened. I'd half-hoped they'd
ignore it; at the same time I wanted their sympathy. But I never quite
knew how they'd react. In this case they were worried and upset and
slightly disbelieving. It was almost as if *I'd* done something wrong. After
intensive questioning, they took me to a specialist who said I should wear
a corset to straighten my spine. Fortunately, my parents disagreed, and a
physiotherapist prescribed exercises which eased the pain.

As I grew older, my back still 'went', usually without warning. The first
sharp surge of pain was a shock, but by rubbing in Tiger Balm I kept
myself mobile, and after a few weeks it usually improved. But as the
attacks became more severe I adapted, arranging my computer so I could
lie on the floor with the screen visible and the keyboard across my knees,
using lots of painkillers and cushions, and sometimes receiving in bed
when friends came around. That way, I could wait out the pain. It didn't
occur to me that a day might come when it would completely take over.

That morning in bed I felt a grinding sensation in my back. It was as if

I'd dried out and there were cracks opening up inside my body. There were wires in my side and my left leg was throbbing. It was so painful it backgrounded everything – even the fear I felt. I'd no idea that illness could hurt so much.

Over the next two months I got used to lying in bed. I didn't have any choice. My body was in spasm and each time I moved the pain levels doubled. I also got used to crying like a child, crawling to the toilet on my hands and knees and eating on my side in bed. I had help, of course. My mother, children and friends all visited and sometimes slept over. The doctor examined me and prescribed painkillers, saying I needed specialist attention, but it was the Thatcher era and because of 'bed blocking' the hospital couldn't take me.

When I was on my own I had to have everything within reach – food, water, pills, phone – and since I slept with the mattress on the floor, the space beside the bed was soon littered. I remember twisting sideways to grab for pills and spilling water and food. I also remember observing myself, looking down from above and seeing the body of a sadhu or an abused prisoner. But the hardest part was getting through the pain. I couldn't believe that my body could bear it. Although I'd been told I had a slipped disc, I kept picturing broken glass and terminal conditions. I imagined my left leg being amputated or my back snapping in half. Words like 'torture' and 'suffering' kept popping into my head.

Being in continuous pain changed who I was. Outwardly, I was tearful and self-pitying, confused at times, and frightened of my pills. I'd become a 'weakie', confined to bed and unable to look after myself. But inside I was calculating how to hang on, counting slowly when the pain was at its worst. I knew that when it peaked, it would ease off afterwards, so counting got me through. At other times I pictured myself underwater, going with the flow. I fantasised about being washed out to sea and surviving inside an air bubble.

I was eventually taken into A&E because the disc was compressing the nerve to my bladder. I remember when the paramedics put me in a chair and carried me downstairs. Inside I was white-hot. Outside, I was shouting like a madman. Afterwards, stretched out in the ambulance, I wept. That was when I began to feel abandoned. I had a friend with me, but I'd lost all connection. My leg was stick-thin, I'd aged twenty years and life didn't seem real or important any more. I was on my way to hospital and there was nothing I could do.

During my time in St Thomas's I adopted the role of patient, adjusting to a sealed space where life slowed down. Looking back, it reminds me of the suspension I felt reading children's books. Hospital is a place set apart, a dream experience where people come and go and decisions are taken as if you were someone else. There's a strangeness about it, an unreal emptiness, so that things appear as if they were on screen — with you as the audience.

I also learned that in hospital nothing is private. Your condition is out there, written all over you, and your carers, however discreet, send out messages about loss and damage. In my case, I didn't care too much about being on show. I'd been exposed on a trolley for eight hours before being wheeled into a ward where everyone could see me. All that mattered was having a bed, the nurses were attentive and the drugs softened everything. Under their influence I slept through for the first time in months — and when I woke, I wasn't hurting.

My pain soon returned, but the drugs helped. I felt cushioned and absorbed; half-awake in a world of sheets and charts and metal-framed beds. A milk-white haze seemed to fill the ward. I could have been a ghost, or someone's imaginary friend.

I still had symptoms, of course. My body felt rubbed raw inside. It was as if all the padding had been sucked out. When I looked down at my left leg I could see the muscles twitching. The leg itself was all skin and bone. But I was able to move, changing position inch by inch, and then with help, to a trolley. The doctors had warned me that I'd have to be tested. Although I knew what was coming, it felt dangerous, especially when I was injected with dye into my spine. I was afraid it would be too much to bear. But after the first shock it became more like a hot flannel, applied from behind. It even felt quite soothing ...

The resulting scan showed a disintegrated disc very low down, one I was told later was a record-breaking size. It led to my move, soon afterwards, to the National Hospital for Neurosurgery where I was taken to theatre within a week. That was another life-changing experience. It taught me about what happens when your body takes over, entering an extreme state, and you drop to the bottom. Years later it helped me to 'get alongside' someone I loved when, after protracted suffering, her body finally gave out and she came close to death ...

I first met Frieda through a friend. We visited her flat at the top of a Victorian terrace near Holloway Road. Frieda was in recovery so it took some time before we heard her on the answerphone. She sounded hoarse and slightly shaky. Having been admitted, we climbed a narrow, dark staircase between flaking walls that doubled back to her door. Frieda opened it and the light shone in from upstairs. Repeating our names she invited us in, and we climbed some more stairs to a landing. Frieda led, holding onto the banisters and wheezing slightly. She was large-bodied and strong, yet her hands were slight and delicate. I remember her moving side to side, using the banisters as handholds, and the sweat running down her head. But I could also see her poise and balance, as she picked her way up like the Kudu she admired. At the top she hugged us, saying she'd heard a lot about me, and led in to the living room. It was full of old furniture covered with dyed cloths and pictures of family and friends on shelves and cupboards. There were low wooden tables cluttered with letters and TV magazines. Potted plants lined the windowsill. In one corner, an ancient computer and printer were gathering dust. After serving tea, Frieda introduced me to the people in her photos, telling me who they were and where they came from. I could see that people meant a lot to her.

That afternoon Frieda told us stories about being brought up on a Namibian farm. Laughing and calling herself 'naughty cow', she talked about chasing runaway animals, getting drunk and playing tricks on her family — mostly to keep up with dares from older children. She talked about her parents — how they reacted by telling her off, but then by talking to her. I could see how she took after them.

One story she told was about the Sixties, living under Apartheid. As a result of U.N. sponsorship Frieda was the only black student in an all-white school. By then, she was a young, critically-aware person and the police were watching her because her white boyfriend was smuggling S.W.A.P.O. activists out of the country. One day the dreaded Koevoet turned up at Frieda's home, and took her off, wedged between two agents in the back of their car. Driving to the cemetery, they parked between two empty graves. Looking meaningfully down at the holes in the ground they demanded to know where her boyfriend was. Frieda was shaking, but she refused to tell them. What followed was unexpected. The driver went into a building to make a telephone call and when he returned, drove the car home in silence.

The explanation, as her friend pointed out, was the U.N. sponsorship. If they'd killed her it would have been a media scandal, and that might have tipped the balance in favour of sanctions against South Africa. But for Frieda it led to her exile. From then on, the police parked daily outside her house, obliging her parents to have her smuggled out to England for her own safety.

For most of her life in England Frieda was ill. She survived type one diabetes, chronic arthritis and two heart attacks, holding out until her third cancer. When I took her into the Whittington Hospital she knew all the staff, mainly because she'd spent time in at least half the departments. She and I shared a joke that her hospital file had a place in the *Guinness Book of Records*. It was so large, we said, that when she changed clinics it had to be moved by wheelbarrow. Another Frieda joke, as she became increasingly housebound, was to call herself 'The Queen', holding court and pretending we were her subjects.

She was warm, expressive and true to herself, and it was her openness to the world that kept her going. So she'd talk to anyone on the street about the weather, politics, sport — anything to connect. With nurses and doctors she'd make friends or fall out — but if she did disagree, usually with good reason, she'd soon find a way of making up. And she stayed in touch with family and friends on the phone, swopping stories and listening to their problems. It was this determination to stay in the world that kept her alive.

I wrote this poem about her.

### In the manor born

You call yourself Queen.

On the phone we talk health,
this week's appointments, tests in clinic,
then matchscore, chances and behaviour in the field.

Your body couldn't hold.
Closing twice, it put you through pain and morphine
and partial recovery, then broke down again
— this time worse — kept you near the edge
of giving up, and even (recovered) still refused duties,
going down often in hypo or fall.

Blue blood, perhaps?
Or birth sign, example and something in the manner?
And you, in your room, lady of the house
with telephone and alarm, plant pots and photos
and cards on the table.
Then waving from the window with a lucky stars smile.

For a day.

The next poem describes her struggle to climb the stairs returning home from a stay in hospital. I'd be close behind, in position to break her fall. As she hauled herself up we'd keep chatting as a deliberate distraction, often talking sport which was one of her passions. In fact, seeing sporting people stretched to the limits made sense to her. As the poem suggests, when it came to illness she was a top performer. And watching T.V. sport both gave her a purpose and filled up time. It was a test, something to excel in, and she followed it closely, as compulsive fun. So she had her 'ins' and 'outs', knew about form and history, and when the England team lost she'd joke about fines and sackings and beating them with crutches.

In her teenage years she'd represented her country, running against South Africa.

### Coming home

She leads.

The key, the hallway, old letters and flyers,
stairs to the top.

One step, then another.

Leading, best foot, for the record,
the attempt is on.

I'm at her shoulder, supporting.

And this is route one.
The here-we-go-again,

first touch, hold on,
to drag up from the bottom.

At bad light, she declares.

The landing creaks.
On turnaround, it worsens.

The top flight is somehow, anyhow,
hands up and scramble
to win against life.

She leads. I follow.

The third poem describes how she learned to live with her multiple conditions, treating them as a marker, something special to her that made her what she was:

## *Ways of being ill*

You're expert at this.

You practise daily on the walk to the shops
with wall-sits, breathless, and waits for the lights.
On the rides around with friends, fronting the bus.
In the pill packs with blisters, 3 x 10, morning, noon and night.
In day-sleeps and sweats and twitches undercover.
In heroics (those small acts large, roped
and connected by exact positioning).
By clock-watch, counting, and marks on the calendar.
And by doing it in turns, in ones, inch-wise, just as it comes up.

It becomes you.

Everything around you has changed.
The walk, the pain. Your bodyweight, falling.
Names of conditions. The effort put in
on good days and bad days and shopping days
and the time spent waiting for the taxi
when the legs give out and the walk ends
stranded on a wall
or a chair in a corner in the chemist.

You're inside, breathing, making it your own.

Returning to your flat,
you're foot down, climbing, hand against plaster,
on the long route to the top,
while upstairs, waiting, your room's in the clear,
lit by the beams of the on-high brightness
where another self looks down
observing from the ceiling
as if this never happened.

Looking back to that first meeting seems to call up all the others. I see
Frieda smiling, next to a plant, gazing out from photo we keep in the
lounge. I picture her in scenes from her flat. She's the short-haired,
round-cheeked woman with a slightly flattened face sitting on the sofa,
talking about childhood. In my head I'm by her side, watching her long
thin fingers fashioning necklaces out of threaded beads. When she'd
strung them and admired them, she gave them all away. I remember her
crosswords and spot-the-ball competitions, her clown-like gestures and

animal noises, her dislike of heat and being told what to do. Most of all I remember her courage.

She was on her third cancer when a carer called me to her house. When I arrived, I found her crouched on the stairs in a state of collapse. While we waited for the ambulance I talked about breathing and counting — and remained in touch. Frieda had been in pain all night and had fallen while descending to the door. She was only half conscious, like an injured climber. I held her hands as if we were about to say our vows. I was with her in her crisis, doing what I could.

I followed the ambulance to the Whittington and sat in A&E until she was given morphine and admitted to a ward, where she slept. I talked, of course, stroking her forehead, and mediating between her and the doctors by explaining any medical terms as best I could. Mostly, I simply kept her company. It was the beginning, although I didn't know it, of a rite of passage. There was a slow, calm inevitability about it, an invisible shift from one place to another.

For a while in hospital, Frieda seemed to improve. When I visited with my present wife Sue, she talked quietly and smiled a little, so we began to believe that she'd somehow pull through. But the cancer was inoperable and when we heard that she'd been moved to a hospice it was a shock, though not unexpected. We visited three times. On the first visit she was barely conscious, wired up with tubes, and we talked quietly about love. She did respond briefly, almost as an aside, speaking about being 'in and out of the proper place'. On the second visit she was in horrible pain, throwing up black bile into a bowl held close to her mouth. When she'd finished vomiting I gave her a little water, but the retching began again. We both held on to her by the shoulders, the back, and by the arms. That was the best we could do. Beneath the sheets her stomach was bloated with cancer.

On the third visit her eyes were closed, her face had softened and she was almost smiling. Her tubes were gone and she looked young again. Her arms were crossed and her body was stretched out. She was dead.

What sustained Frieda for so long was hope. Even in her final stay in hospital she was still optimistic, talking about going back home and flying to Namibia. She remained jolly and engaged, even in pain, and when it hurt too much she called out, "Ay-ay-ay," or she squeezed herself forward into a ball, breathing hard — and then carried on. The runner in her kept going, regardless. And each time she fell, she picked herself up and redoubled her efforts. She was fearless and loving and spent her life in training for the big moment still to come. It was all part of her connectedness, and her will to live.

Frieda had told me that she nearly died on the operating table: once during pancreatic surgery, the second time during a heart operation. In a minor way, I experienced something similar during surgery at the National Hospital for Neurosurgery.

It began with anaesthetic, taking effect as an orderly wheeled me through double doors. I remember being shut down but still conscious, struggling in a black hole in my head. It only lasted seconds but it reminded me of an L.S.D. experience years earlier where I'd rolled on the floor with sparks shooting through my brain. That time I'd heard people for what seemed hours walking above me, stepping on my grave – but this time the talk soon cut out, turning into blackout.

It was a six-hour operation. In my mind there's a picture of a blue-lit room with figures in white leaning over a body in a sheet. The angle is from the doorway and it's slightly blurred, but they could be angels gathered at a tomb. Of course it's only a picture, with the sound turned down to a whisper, so it could be invented – but it has the power of flashbulb memory. I imagine this is what people go through when they talk about 'near death experiences'.

When I woke from the operation I felt raw all over, as if my insides had been sandpapered. I stayed in recovery for a couple of hours, drinking and sweating, then returned to the ward and slept. When I woke I rolled over without thinking and tensed, expecting the worst. But my back felt suddenly light and comfortable; it had regained its flexibility, and it didn't hurt ...

The relief after illness brings up feelings that run deep. I've seen this in people with chronic conditions who struggle through months of darkness then light up at a minor act of kindness. Their joy, which might seem disproportionate, is actually small compared with what they've been through. In my case, it took some time before the recovery kicked in. I'd seen the other patients, who needed brain surgery, bandaged like crash victims, but despite their blood loss and starey looks, they survived. They were in the front line, holding themselves together, and to see what they went through, like Frieda, gave made me courage. If they could get better then so could I.

To recover is a gift. What's called homeostasis[1] works in the mind as well as the body. It's about taking risks, giving yourself up and allowing freefall while watching for the break, the very small shift that leads to change. It goes with staying in touch, being present and living through the pain.

I was given physiotherapy exercises for my back. Practising them daily gradually restored my health. I was lucky that my life came back, and the ageing process went into reverse. But I didn't forget what it had been like to be helpless.

I had one more extreme illness experience. It happened on my honeymoon with Sue. All week, my sides had been achingly tender, and although I'd used embrocation and painkillers, nothing really helped. I also found myself — whether through pain, lack of sleep or some sort of prescience — increasingly fatigued. I'd been feeling particularly worn that day and when we reached our Gîte, I lay down on the bed. But then I felt a deep inner heat inside my body, as if something serious was coming. Of course it could have been my mind-set, but what happened then was very physical, quite extraordinary and beyond my control.

The heat flowed up my body from feet to head. When it reached my heart I found myself palpitating and struggling for breath. Although there was nothing I could do, I wasn't in panic or hyperventilating. Sue was by my side and I was telling her calmly what was happening, almost as if I was speaking about someone else. I'd reached a point where it seemed that any moment now I might pass away.

There were three attacks. Arriving in waves, they completely took over. Something powerful was in there, working through my body; it was hot, caustic and overwhelming. This was something that couldn't be denied.

The ambulance was delayed, so by the time I was tested it was too late to diagnose, but the hospital suggested shingles. When I got home, after trawling the Internet and talking with my doctor, I formed a theory that what I'd been through was septic shock — a life-threatening illness where the autoimmune system lashes out to defend against invading bacteria. In this case the 'enemy' was probably shingles plus some other bug. The rest of my body got caught in the crossfire.

I'd learned already from Frieda that the same condition affects people

---

1 The tendency of a system, especially the physiological system of higher animals, to maintain internal stability, owing to the coordinated response of its parts to any situation or stimulus that would tend to disturb its normal condition or function.

differently. Like plants, the exact shade varies, even amongst the same variety. I'd seen the same in friends with good days, bad days, flare-ups and remissions and a whole range of symptoms, some aggressive, some to be expected and some quite surprising. And I saw it again, this time *in extremis* with Chris, my colleague from work, and her leukaemia.

I first met Chris in my teachers' training class at college. She'd been accrediting cleaners for years and didn't see the point in writing essays about what she knew already. She was chunky, red-haired and formidable, but secretly lacking in confidence and easily put off. We had an unspoken agreement that when she tried I'd give her lots of praise and when she lost patience I'd divert her with a joke. She passed, receiving her certificate, and when I stepped down as a manager we often found ourselves using the same staffroom. Chris enjoyed joshing — a game I learned to play from her — but behind her verbal sparring she was a warmly caring, passionate woman with a supportive family.

When she went into hospital her red blood cell count was dangerously low. Within days it regenerated, then dropped again. The pressures of illness seemed to fire her up. She was ghostly-white, refusing food and objecting to her treatment. Part of her believed that the hospital was out to poison her. The chemo, she said, made everything yellow and, "Disgusting. Like chewing bloody rubber." She was shouty, couldn't bear being cooped up and swore a lot at the nurses.

I didn't visit often but I kept in touch by email, writing pieces about daylight, nature and the garden. She thanked me, calling me a poet, and asked for more. For a while I emailed twice a day, but as her condition worsened I changed to text, calling her 'Wonder Woman' and 'Lara Croft' and saying she was a toughie who couldn't be beaten. When she was discharged I messaged about Jailhouse Rock and blasting her way out. We built up a story: she was Crazy Woman Chris who couldn't be caged. Whatever the illness she would ride it and fight it and smash her way through. So when her ex biked her to the sea, I messaged about Steppenwolf and doing a ton, and when she returned to hospital I texted she'd soon bust down the walls and force her way out. It was a necessary fiction, one we both believed in. It raised her energy levels and gave her belief. My job, as her poet and director, was to keep up the action.

The last time I saw her was at her house. She'd been discharged, but in line with our story, I told her they'd *had* to release her. In fact she was bedridden. Her voice was thin and her body emaciated. She'd become greyly worn, so flat in the bed she was almost invisible. Whatever I said at that point was a gesture, a kind of last-ditch rallying cry and final salute.

Her funeral service was pagan. There were pictures of water on rocks with words about spirit-life and wholeness and a talk about essence and return. She was still Chris, the Witch or White Goddess, become one with nature. It was the inner thread that held her. But I knew how long her desperate, crazy stubbornness had kept her alive. In my mind I heard: *Do not go gentle into that good night* ...

After knowing Chris and Frieda, I shouldn't have been surprised when I first experienced age-related illness. I was past 60, so some sort of 'condition' was to be expected. But what I hadn't foreseen was how difficult it would be to diagnose.

My problem began as I walked uphill in the Surrey hills. It was a long, steep slope, and as I climbed, both ankles and the soles of my feet began to ache. By the time I arrived home I was in acute pain. My legs wouldn't carry me and I went to bed with hot water bottles and painkillers. I feared it might be my back again, but then I recalled a similar episode when I'd been suddenly laid up with my ankles burning. It had come and gone, without obvious cause, as a three-day wonder. I'd been alarmed, but after taking time off work, I'd soon recovered.

This attack was different. The pain spread, knotting my muscles, and stiffening between my shoulder blades. My lower neck ached, my arms tingled and my sleep was fitful, broken by cramps. Climbing the stairs was exhausting: my legs didn't work and I had to haul myself up by the banisters. It was as if I was being gripped from inside by a strange kind of paralysis.

After a few days I went out for a walk. It was slow and painful and I found myself shuffling. There was stumpiness about my movement as if I was out of practice. My body ached, my legs were heavy and my rhythm was lost. I seemed to be losing touch with my physical self.

The tests showed nothing. I didn't have vitamin deficiencies, arthritis, diabetes, anaemia or various kinds of joint or connective problems. My brain scan for MS was clear and the consultant warned me that it wasn't worth pursuing other neurological conditions.

So today, as I write, I'm dealing with something that doesn't show in tests, no one can name, and only exists as a theory. It's a limbo state with only one witness. More than that, when my condition changes and my mobility improves, it raises suspicions that really, with nothing visible, I must be faking. People expect illness to be either steady and measured, like walking, or a sudden collapse. But whatever I've got is both persistent and extreme. In fact, for me, the bad times and good times take turns, and I'm in the middle, listening to my body, judging my response, practising my footwork ...

So what have I learned?

The lack of a diagnosis doesn't matter. It's about running your own race and finding a way through.

To articulate helps. So writing this piece is a lift; it names my problem as something-like-what-I-say.

There are so many conditions. They overlap and mimic. And this is just one, as yet unnamed.

It's never final. Right now, like Frieda and Chris, I'm alive and kicking.

Illness is creative. Every day brings a new discovery.

There are so many ways to cope, each one unique to the person getting help.

Illness changes everything. Suddenly there are questions. What used to happen easily requires hours of practice and what you once took for granted now seems impossible. As pain takes over the body reacts and fear and doubt close down options. A wall goes up and the world out there begins to seem dangerous.

And the questions go deep. They can put you on the spot, or change you completely. And to find ways to handle them, to know what's coming and sidestep or adapt, is part of what you learn. So when the voices take over, asking, 'Am I the same person?' and, 'Is this really happening?' that's when it's good to take a break and talk. Because illness isn't linear; there's no pre-set sequence and it doesn't follow formula. More often, like mine, it's outside the categories and hard to read. The trick is to stay open and accept guidance, particularly from doctors, while searching for methods that work for you.

So, while going through tests, I spent time in counselling, discussing my condition. It wasn't about cures or fixes or finding simple answers. My counsellor drew diagrams and talked biology, but mostly it was imaginative. Her focus was on insight and being mindful of what we say, especially to ourselves. She talked about compassion, directing our thoughts and sharing positives. Being with her gave me an awareness, an in-the-body method using words of affirmation and steady breathing — and her own very real experience of MS.

So here's what she came up with:

♪ Body and mind are indivisible. All conditions are affected by thought.
♪ Smile and be positive, it helps.
♪ Avoid, *should've, would've, could've.*
♪ Energy follows thought.
♪ Remember the plasticity of the brain. Feed it good stuff: it will rewire.
♪ Pain is information, not necessarily a problem.

♪ The body has its own nervous system, a kind of mini-brain. It needs to be listened to.
♪ Ask yourself, what is my body telling me today?
♪ Muscles have fear.
♪ Relax, don't panic. It triggers fight/flight/freeze.
♪ Walk naturally and breathe from the stomach.
♪ When it's a struggle: stop, take stock and notice the difference. Then start afresh.
♪ Relearn movement with baby steps.
♪ Remind yourself, even in pain you always have a choice.
♪ Play with the notion that you might, or might not, do things.
♪ Live in the moment.
♪ Tell yourself quietly not to be afraid, you can do it.
♪ See illness as a gift. It shows who you are.

*Genre becomes literature when it questions appearances and shows what's inside.*

*Writing mustn't splurge or gush. The feelings may spark but the heat they generate has to be contained.*

*What we consider good in the expressive arts is always up for debate. A healthy culture welcomes new ideas on who we are or might be.*

# 7th MOVEMENT

# EXPRESSION RULES

**What readers said about:**
*The True History of Purple*
*The Purpose of Poetry*
*Chris Hill Interviews Leslie Tate*
*Creative Spark*   and   *Family Album*

It is wonderful and truly inspiring to read such an honest account of the development both of a novel and, in parallel, a writer, and to be able to watch the creative process unfold on the page. Leslie Tate courageously reveals a process which is too often hidden from the world. New writers often feel that there must be a secret magic formula which, if only the established authors would share it, would give them the key that unlocks the mystery of writing. I think Leslie Tate's account comes as close I've ever read to revealing that strange alchemical process.

There are some lines in his story which have sent my own imagination reeling '... the book created an alternative version of my own experience, a kind of theatre of possibilities ...' And 'A sentence is bridge and there is a limit to how much weight it can bear.' Like the Russian nesting dolls those lines have whole stories and poems buried inside them. And if an author's words can set another writer or artist afire with new ideas, as these do for me, then that is creativity at its blazing best.

— *Karen Maitland Author of Company of Liars, The Owl Killers, The Gallows Curse, Falcons of Fire and Ice, The Vanishing Witch and The Raven's Head.*

*Expression Rules* is a beautiful and engaging read, which manages to be intensely personal without descending into self-absorption. If, to use a cliché, it takes the reader on a journey, it's one which takes a most scenic route. The author's love of language shines through, and it's a love affair which has clearly grown and deepened over time, as his appreciation of its subtlety and power has evolved.

I found Leslie Tate's description of the process of writing, and in particular how his own craft developed, both insightful and thought-provoking; not least in terms of how that very process can awaken one's own self-awareness in a far wider context. Crucially, it holds out the hand of hope to aspirant authors who

may be struggling with uncertainty and a lack of confidence in their ability: the label of 'writer' can be earned not just by those with 'innate ability', but also through patient and persistent toil, learning one's craft in the old-fashioned way, reflecting constantly both on one's work and oneself, and having faith ...
— *Cat Turner, Author, Speaker and Eco-Activist.*

In our rushed society we are at risk of forgetting to appreciate the things that are wondrous — writing, music, art, the creative spark in its many forms; so many things considered only worthy if we can put a price on them. Leslie Tate's writing gently reminds us to step back and appreciate; and he clarifies beautifully the paradox that novels don't just fall out on the page, but take hours and hours of patient care, editing and wordsmithery to make them appear that way.
— *Izzy Robertson, Author and Health Professional.*

This really resonated with me as a writer, especially editing out thousands of words and working eight hours a day on a manuscript and being forced to come to terms with why you are writing at all. The whole section was very enjoyable.
— *Amanda Thow, Author and Counsellor.*

# THE TRUE HISTORY OF *PURPLE*

If a book is an adventure, then writing it is a shot in the dark. And in the case of the novel I wanted to write, it seemed to have a mind of its own. So when I started *Purple*[1] in 2006 I had no idea of where I was going or what might come up.

Don Paterson compares a poem to a child, growing with the help of the writer until it can stand on its own feet. In his words, it 'starts as wholly yours and slowly ceases to become so'. So, after years of work the book or poem takes its place in the adult world, independent of its author.

The child analogy implies that a book has an intrinsic value that goes beyond the question 'What's it worth?' It cannot be exchanged for something simpler or more accessible without loss, and the precise choice of words makes it quick and alive in its own special way. So the book I wanted to write had a voice of its own and a subversive relationship to the modern world, it was to be based on language and character and would move the reader — most of all it would be a grown-up read, a reflective piece which *is of itself*, more a novel than a gap-filler.

I began writing from what the comedians call a point of view. I'd gone up to college in the late Sixties, making myself visible on 'the scene', but behind the mask I was still a solitary boy, bullied at school and very afraid of sexual contact, about which I knew nothing. I used that contradiction to flesh out my first sentence, which took me four days to jiggle and juggle until I finally fixed all I knew about the novel into 33 words ... 'As a young man, beginning at college what he'd later describe as his "Hendrix days", Matthew Lavender took pride in his newfound ability to understand others, diagnosing their problems by extension from himself.' Later, I rationalised it as my big jump start, switching the reader into a different historical era, but at the same time I was learning how to write complex sentences while easing myself into character and feel. I was hearing the start of my own, individual voice as a novelist.

Beginning in third person held me at a distance from the events I'd lived through, giving the characters room to breathe and be themselves. And I soon found that my presence as both author and protagonist became a

---

1 Publication dates: Purple Oct 2015, Blue Nov 2016 and Violet 2017.

guide, keeping it on track emotionally without taking over. In the past, whenever I'd sat down to write I'd not been equal to the task, the great authors were beyond me, no plot twists or bookish ideas presented and there was only personal experience staring me in the face.

But as I pushed through, writing two or three hundred words a day and discarding thousands more, I soon came to realise that it was impossible to write from life. A character in a book follows much tighter, more constrained patterns than people in their changeable and often contradictory lives. And novels select, often recombining experience, or extending a half-forgotten anecdote into something larger and more generic than the source material. I also found that writing gives you a vocabulary to map parts of the self you didn't know existed.

The book is bigger than the author. The first one I produced, which was the prototype for *Purple*, took two years to write, working about eight hours each day. It charted the coming-of-age of Matthew Lavender as he learned the hard way from a series of gradually deepening relationships. With only the characters to guide me I wrote myself into tight corners where the way out depended on some small detail or a chance remark. Often these 'saves' had to be backed up retrospectively by adding a few subtle pointers in the lead-up, but they brought life into the writing. If I didn't know what was going to happen next, neither would the reader. But it wasn't about throwing in arbitrary cliff-hangers to spice up the action; each incident was intended to be a small, surprising case study showing what people are like.

When my first book was remaindered without warning I was forced to come to terms with why I was writing. I'd realised already that when agents and publishers talked about the bottom line they meant selling the T.V./film rights to a book. I wasn't writing to please a particular readership and what was respected in literary circles was either elaborate, theory-driven narrative switches or heavily-edited prose based on one prototype: the stripped-down language of Hemingway and Carver. My problem with the first was that it lacked the emotional authenticity to engage at deeper levels, and the second had become, in the hands of creative writing courses, a narrow, worked-out orthodoxy. What I hadn't encountered at that time was the evangelical editor who feels compelled to red-line every sentence in the interests of cleanliness and economy. My publishers were more the basic error-proofing type, with a greater interest in my 'contributory payment' than the quality of the writing, but they weren't vanity press because they rejected manuscripts. What they did do was charge for publication then, after a couple of years, send me a registered letter containing a certificate and a short explanatory statement. It informed me that they'd already taken my novel out of circulation.

In the year that followed I kept my book alive by purchasing author copies, but in the end both that novel and my second, the prototype for *Blue*, were remaindered. So I had to face it: I called myself a poet and a novelist, yet without any books I had to nothing to prove it. Of course we all dream, but how can anyone claim they're a writer when they have no readers? It made me ask the question: *Why Write* — or why write at all? Was it about money or being admired? Or was it, as I'd heard many authors say, purely for entertainment? Did I have to please my target audience? And if I had one, should I play them with teasing plot tricks to keep them awake or fill up the pages with what they wanted to hear?

Sue Hampton and I often give joint presentations as husband and wife and *Authors in Love*. In sessions where we've asked audiences *Why Write?* we've found that most people think of writing as personal therapy or a fall-back career. So we put some cards together to explain our beliefs. They read:

Why do we write?
1. Because it's what we do best.
2. Because readers deserve a variety of writing.
3. To explore the big themes that matter most — like love, power, change and freedom.
4. Because we have to, it's our passion.
5. Because words can change how you see the world.
6. To make people think and feel.
7. Because we have a wonderful language, which we value (so try to make it fun, stretch it, make it count).
8. Because a story can take you into a different world you may never visit, and make you part of it.
9. Because a great story is an experience you never forget and it can become part of who you are.
10. Because a story can help you understand yourself and other people.
11. Because a strongly-drawn character can stay with you for the rest of your life.
12. Because we've been inspired by great writers.

The cards didn't generate enough discussion so we abandoned them, but I did come up with a different *Why Write* formula — one to help authors when faced with isolation and loss of self-esteem. It comes in three parts and goes like this:
a) A writer is never alone. The voice of the author is intersectional, imitating dialogue and group phrases from out there, while charting

an authentic personal monologue. So the narrator talks to the audience as well as the self; and the task is to find the words that spark feelings across these two worlds.

b) In that context 'accessibility' or 'relatability' is not the aim. The reader is involved in piecing together something unfamiliar and yet recognisable through the conventions of stories.

c) Nevertheless, writing is a lonely, time-consuming task involving constant revisions. To keep it up requires a deliberate, strategic 'tuning out' of criticism while remaining sharply critical of every detail. As any top sportsperson will tell you, work hard on your weaknesses while telling yourself you can go all the way.

But my belief in the quality of my writing didn't hold up when I returned to my first remaindered novel. I realised it needed the blue pencil. So I removed the phrases that I'd put in to reinforce my meaning, and shortened the introductions to changes of time and place. I'd been too careful, trying to ease the reader in and 'signposting' things that I'd half-said or implied already. It needed a lighter, quicker touch, fewer adjectives and more flow. On the other hand, I found myself adding in phrases to smooth the transition between mood changes. I did so to avoid the pared-down, all-action kind of writing where characters go through extreme experiences without, apparently, being touched by them. I also filled in gaps where the scene jumped, missing out an obvious emotional step in the development of the protagonist's feelings. I was busy stripping back, filling the holes and making good.

Writing is a slow, hermetic exploration of your own limits. And the opportunity to revise a novel is a building process where each added layer cements the last, bonding it together and strengthening the whole. What emerges is more than the personality of the author. So my novel had already taught me that the Sixties was a high-risk era for young people like me. We'd been brought up as 'straights' and now we looked down on our former selves, scorning our parents' values and dosing ourselves up with dangerous drugs. But behind the hip mask most of us were out of our depth. And in my case, the fear of sex, backed up by my secret crossdressing, added to the sense of being 'out of it'. As a trans person, the danger of discovery placed me in a category of one. But that also gave me a subject to write about: my bildungsroman of the peace and love era. Because we all had an emotional hole to fill — some like me needed to deny our fathers, others were hedonists, a few were crazy — and we all felt unequal to the goals our society had set us.

It was during the edit of my book that a new idea came up. I realised that there was a persistent immaturity about Matthew, and that to interleave his grandmother's experience from an earlier generation would add depth to the story. But writing her in required a different skillset. Mary's tale, told in first person, contrasts to Matthew's in that the sentences are shorter, key words and expressions are drawn from my North East England background and there are no colons, semi-colons, dashes or ellipses. But the real significance of Mary is that she's brought up, like I was, to be different. My parents were fiercely and proudly oppositional, so I was told to stand out, 'be my own person' and take the contrary view. There was a great deal of it about in the apparently conformist Fifties, particularly in the North — and it came from the grandparents.

So what I realised in adding Mary's story was that the individualism of the 'me generation' was inherited from the tribe. It was the same drive, expressed in a very different way that stood what the parents believed in on its head.

I was lucky enough to find a new publisher. They backed *Purple*, allowing it a second life. But even before that, Sue had suggested something that broadened the novel still further. She noticed that Richard, the joint protagonist of my second novel, read like a relation of Matthew's. From that seed grew a family tree of Lavenders. It gave me the chance to link up *Purple* with *Blue*, the renamed second book, and on to *Violet*, the third in the trilogy, written while editing the other two. And the links between stories came to express themselves in various forms — letters, articles and speeches — each with their viewpoint and unique vocal range. I'd spent half my waking life for nine years on the art of writing and my long apprenticeship had finally resulted in *Purple*, *Blue* and *Violet*[1] finding their true colours. I'd learned to take risks, I didn't need to win the reader round, and my immature book that started out as a satirical self-portrait had grown and developed into a character-led window on modern relationships.

So why did I do it? I wanted to shine a clear, unflinching light on the 'swinging Sixties', showing how coolly elitist and vulnerable we really were. I felt the Beat writers of the times ranted too much. For years the voice in my head had been composing a story, turning my 'wow-man' experiences inside out and exploring the psychology behind the hype. But to get it down on paper I had to stop waiting for the magic moment and discipline myself to write every day. When I did, I discovered it was like building a wall: the first words needed to fit exactly, or everything would fall down. I also discovered that the book created an alternative version of my own experience, a kind of theatre of possibilities that seemed more real than anything I remembered. My other discovery was that words will only go as far as you can stretch them and that sometimes you have to cut your losses. A sentence is a bridge and there's a limit to how much weight it can bear. On the other hand, to thin down the language limits what you can say. So I aimed at a balance between long and short sentences, mixing the formal with the spoken, and developed my plot through subtle shifts in the narrative voice.

A novel never ends, it's simply a question of where you cut off. Like life, it's always in motion and yet it remains fixed once it's on the page. So it seemed quite natural to end *Purple* in the magic present, but outside time, on the beach. There were personal reasons, too. My childhood beach was where people 'loosened up', playing games and showing their true feelings. Later, in adolescence, it was a place full of sea and sky and receding horizons that lifted me out of myself. So I ended *Purple* open to the elements, on a high, trusting to luck, and following the line of sound and feel. I'd always been afraid to swim but now I needed to go back to the water and do what I did as child: jump with the waves and shout. And the voice I heard, calling out in fear and excitement, came from the words.

# THE PURPOSE OF POETRY

*We shouldn't talk about what the poem or image means, so much as what meaning it generates*
— Don Paterson

When I was at school poetry was taught by spotting similes, metaphors and other figures of speech. We memorised lines, rote-learning what the poet was 'doing' at various points in the text and copied out prose summaries of our set poems. We were also instructed in sonnet form, syllable-count and meter. It was all about displaying received knowledge and passing exams. Oddly, we didn't think to ask about the purpose of a poem.

Outside the classroom the boys and their parents had a different idea. They believed they knew what a poem was about. It was a kind of puffed-up airy nonsense full of effete gestures and fancy language — either that, or a poem made no sense at all and was not worth the paper it was written on.

Both approaches were summed up by the rhetorical question, 'What's the use of poetry?' Poetry was too much above our heads to be questioned or it was a complete waste of time. So we learned to get on with it in the classroom while admiring more down-to-earth things, like sport or earning money.

But what I remember was a sense of wonder. The similes and metaphors surprised me, and the poems had an inner wildness and strangeness which spoke of other things. And I lived that feeling in the privacy of my bedroom or out walking, making it happen by repeating lines without understanding, casting myself as a Romantic poet and working myself up to a spiritual lather.

The purpose of a poem seems very different to me today. It's closer to jazz or dance or mindful observation. So, what would I say to my younger self about the purpose of poetry?

a.  It doesn't have any purpose at all if you try to measure it by money, work, exams or scoring goals. It can carry a 'message' or help with difficult feelings but its primary function is to be a thing of beauty, an elusive, affirmatory or shocking experience, or a series of surprising expressions which cannot be adequately stated in any other terms.

b.  It does have music. In fact a poem 'stops making sense' only in so far as we require a single, logically-constructed meaning from language. A poem steers a middle path between grammar and the sound of words. So to appreciate its unique voice you have to tune in, rather than irritably demand what on earth it's going on about.

c.  At the same time it can be helpful to trace a thread of meaning through a poem. It won't be exhaustive and there will be ambiguities but it does provide a framework. The flower that grows on that framework is full of scent, colour and texture — and every day it changes.

d.  To interrogate a poem takes a lot of practice. It involves examining words carefully from all sides, trying to plot their moves and measure their connections. It's a matter of feel and practice and knowing their backgrounds and habits. It can involve the skills of a tracker.

e.  Poems are about metaphor. Recognising new similarities in a complex world.

So taking apart a poem can be genuinely helpful if it offers a structure for thought and feeling that can be discarded later. The problem I have with my schooling was that by concentrating purely on technical effects we missed the heart of the poem. In our reductive, literalist classroom we were missing the sense of strangeness, of deep connection and surprising meanings. Instead of allowing the poem to interpret us, we had the task of boxing up the poem and fitting it to a practical formula, one that would allow us to 'pass' our tests. So the purpose was external, quite lacking in the reflective or transformative process that poetry can and should initiate.

I'd like to finish with a poem of mine which describes the hunt for words facing a blank sheet of paper, until the right expression, the simplest, appears. It's about the inner, hard-to-reach nature of the poem and the possible 'ghost' poems that lie behind the finished work. It could have been titled: *Creation Ex Nihilo*.

### Hunt the poem

Close your eyes.

Can you touch blank? A sheet without thickness?

Feel around the base, the sides,

finger-test substance to imprint in air?

Name it for likeness, background, element and mix.

Try one way, try another. Peel off string and wrappers

to weigh, take samples and bouquet.

Egg-raw, chewy, fired-up, piquant.

Or truth grains, stalks and a lump in the throat.

Now open, slowly,

to music, sunlight in mirrors,

a door knock and footsteps in the hall

and a bird in the hand.

# CHRIS HILL INTERVIEWS LESLIE TATE

http://www.chrishillauthor.co.uk/

**Chris:** Tell me a little bit about yourself as a person.

**Leslie:** I'm romantic and driven, with a love of music, people and the written word.

**Chris:** Tell me about your journey as a writer — how you started and how you have developed.

**Leslie:** At university in the late Sixties I skipped lectures in favour of taking drugs, absorbing myself in experimental music and reading art books and literature till four in the morning. I 'discovered' Webster, Flaubert, Kafka, Rimbaud and Basho for myself. It made me feel special being 'into' writers other people had never heard of. But behind my crazy hip mask I was a sexual innocent whose poetry was as narcissistically immature as my public persona. At the time I wanted to be a writer but I was in too much awe of what F.R. Leavis called The Great Tradition, so I took to 'warehousing' experience, storing my impressions for later use. As in the story of St Augustine, I kept promising to change and sit down to write my novel BUT NOT YET.

There were three landmarks after university. The first was during an M.A. in Creative Writing at Goldsmiths' College, London, in the Eighties when I realised that inspiration from above wasn't going to happen. I discovered, by reading the biographies of several writers, that lyrical, flowing pieces were often the result of slow, patient, line-by-line work, going on for weeks or years. It helped me to get over the feeling that I couldn't write because it didn't come naturally, and so I schooled myself to the business of endless revision. Nowadays, for every word on the page I've tried and rejected ten others. The second landmark was meeting my present wife, Sue Hampton, in 2006, and reading her books. Understanding her writing, which has a classic feel, showed me how the extended prose line is more tied together by meaning than poetry. But I knew from poetry that sound makes absolute sense, so I still test for rhythm and cadence, reading 'out loud in my head' when I revise. The third stage involved finding an individual voice, blending the literary with the conversational, writing two published novels and starting a third then attending a University of East Anglia/Guardian Masterclass in 2012.

**Chris:** How would you describe your work — its themes and the important things about it?

**Leslie:** I write about modern love, from tentative and awkward first date to passionate late-life romance. I want to communicate how it feels to be thoughtful and maybe at odds with society and at the same time involved in an intense, challenging love affair or a mistaken marriage. I want to 'look inside the book' and show how much the relationships we see all around us have changed during the 20th century, but as an imaginative act, rather than a historical investigation.

The characters and the words I use shape my books. I don't have a plot in mind, other than a general feel for the people and places I'm portraying. I head straight into the highs and lows of personal experience because I want to show people from the inside, as they are when they're not 'presenting', stripped of inhibition. Of course I know that a novel can only show a fragment of who we are, so I try to steer the book into challenging and deeply-felt incidents I've experienced in order to get to the quick of things. But the books usually get the better of me and lead me into episodes that are equally challenging but belong to the story, rather than me. I often feel like an escape artist when I'm writing because my characters get themselves into fixes that don't seem to offer any easy way out. Fortunately something usually comes to my rescue — a symbolic object or a key remark or a setting comes up where something decisive can happen. If it doesn't then I have to scrub part of the book and start again. If a scene does come together I often find myself going back and writing in pointers to the new element that is going to change the story.

I see writing as a shared journey into the dark with a reflective and transformative purpose.

**Chris:** Tell me about your debut novel — what is it about and what makes it a great read?

**Leslie:** *Purple* is the first in a trilogy. It begins with Matthew Lavender's coming-of-age story, going up to university in 1969 and dating women while hiding his sexual naiveté behind a mask of wildness. His story alternates with his gran Mary describing her harsh 1920's upbringing. Her story offers clues as to why Matthew and his parents are the way they are. The two protagonists come together at the end.

Matthew's section is deep and lyrical, describing the up-and-down, chaotic and posy business of attraction and repulsion between fired-up young people. It's also wildly comic when he escapes to a Sixties-style commune. But I've made sure it's true to life and not full of hype or nostalgia. Mary's section is direct and shocking, showing family conflict and rebellion. Her upbringing is intensely individualistic, a theme that runs through the book. But Mary is a warm, likeable character, an accommodator who sees and shares things that go deep. In both stories I've tried to create fully-rounded characters who change and develop as a result of what they go through.

**Chris:** Tell me about writing *Blue*, the second book in your trilogy. How did it start?

**Leslie:** With *Blue* I'd already decided that I wanted to explore a different type of beginning from *Purple* — a slower, step-by-step approach. So it's a controlled outing, a walk in the park if you like, with enough time to look around. The reader is taken into the lives of Richard and Vanessa gradually, through pacing and changes in voice. And because I wanted to fully explore the action, each incident has an element of stillness, a kind of freeze-frame feel. So the moments of drama extend and elaborate themselves, stretching time and space.

**Chris:** What else, as a writer, went into *Blue*?

**Leslie:** I needed a strong, flexible authorial voice. So I did a lot of rereading and editing until I found a style — a combination of formal and informal, in third person, dipping in and out of my two main characters' heads. But when I revisited the story later, new ideas popped up. For instance a new start, with Richard's cousin, Professor Matthew, lecturing about relationships. His voice was witty and erudite, offering indirect comments on Vanessa and Richard's marital struggles. It added an element of fun and a connection between the books. Other styles appeared, helping to vary the narrative, including articles, dialogues and programme notes for an exhibition. What I'd put together by the end was a collection of voices, all bearing on the same question: can Vanessa and Richard save their marriage?

**Chris:** What would you pick out as the most difficult part to write in *Blue*?

**Leslie:** Probably the counselling scene. I needed one because it's what so many people do if they're having relationship difficulties. But the talking cure has a problem — you can't just have people sitting there for page after page doing nothing. So I deliberately 'packed it in', squeezing hours of talk into a few concentrated exchanges before moving on to practical, slightly wacky exercises. In effect, I condensed several sessions into one, making it possible for Richard and Vanessa to achieve tangible progress. When you're writing that sort of thing, it's the idea that counts — the dream, in a way, of how we might speak if we were free to. As an author I often overlay the actual with the generic like that, striking a balance between the documentary and the imaginary. Mind, it took a lot of editing and inserts to make the writing carry enough charge and detail, to be dramatic enough *and* grounded. The process, as Susan Sontag says, makes the writer, 'Love words, agonize over sentences. And pay attention to the world.'

**Chris:** So how would you categorise *Blue* if you had to? Does it have a genre?

**Leslie:** Lyrical realism or literary, if you like. By literary I mean four things — it's based on character and language, it digs beneath the surface and it includes several types of writing and genres. There's also a 'state of the nation' element. So *Blue* is a historical story told in the form of a satirical-romantic-adventure. It covers that time in life when couples struggle to 'stay alive' against the pressures of jobs and bringing up children. It's also, like *Purple*, an investigation into modern love.

**Chris:** Where can we find out more about you?

**Leslie:** My website is www.leslietate.com. I have two pages on Facebook, a) Leslie Tate Author b) Leslie Stuart Tate. You can find me on Twitter @LSTateAuthor. I like to make friends and share stories with other people.

# THE CREATIVE SPARK

*Any level of guided activity teaches you just how difficult it is to reach mastery.*

I remember several people in my family who were creative. My grandpa on my mother's side was a tenor who, I've been told, was invited to train in Italy but had to turn the opportunity down because he was a railway clerk with a family to support. On a trip to London he recorded his voice at H.M.V., Oxford Street, which had its own studio. Sadly, the 78 r.p.m. disc he produced has gone missing. He conducted the local choir in his N.E. seaside town in performances of *The Messiah*, even changing churches to retain creative control. His wife was a natural accompanist on the piano and also played the organ. They were like fire and water; he was the leader, she gave of herself and supported. Their front room was a busy place with leading members of the choir popping in, and recordings of Beethoven's symphonies rising from the depths of the 'Horn Cabinet' that he and my dad built in the corner.

My granny and grandpa also sang Geordie songs, staged *The Mikado* in full fancy dress, and he performed *Nessun Dorma*. They had their encores, well-known 'pleasers', ranging from Mendelssohn to Flanders and Swann. What they put on was largely determined by provincial taste, but they were also well-informed, subscribing to *The Gramophone* and visiting London for the Proms. Despite having limited practice time, they achieved high standards and were respected in the village as talented folk who could play almost anything. In fact they were traditionalists; they didn't take risks and their repertoire was conventional, but as a boy I greatly admired them.

My dad was very serious about classical music. It didn't come from his family; he was entirely self-taught. He could knock out popular tunes on the piano, but Beethoven was his real love. Unfortunately his tolerance levels were low. So when he first heard Mahler as a result of a programme change at a concert he decided from then on that all modern music was 'rubbish'.

Fixing things was my dad's way of 'making himself useful'. Although he was handy, he wasn't trained and the jobs he did were rather hit and miss.

I have photos of him covered with grease lying under a small black Austin. Afterwards, his hands would be, as my mum said, *cut to ribbons*. He repaired appliances by trial and error and rigged up his own version of double glazing. He was also a hobbyist. So he varnished pictures, was an amateur photographer, played chess and bridge, and started me on Airfix and Meccano models. His father collected beer mats, newspaper clippings and fancy tin boxes. He knew lots of jokes and could recite all the capitals of the world. Granddad was naughty and competitive, cheated at cards and teased his wife.

The women in the family would sit in deckchairs knitting on the beach. They made patchwork rugs, mended clothes, shopped and cooked, baked on tight budgets, and cared for children. My dad's mother brewed fiery ginger beer. The jars stood maturing along a high shelf in her kitchen. Since housework was so much more demanding in those days, their activities were less flamboyant than the men, more bread-and-butter.

True, most of these activities were sex-typed. The men's were practical, often requiring controlled strength, while the women's were decorative or designed for consumption. Some of their efforts were for fun, others resembled occupational therapy, all of them brought people together. In their world the village was the unit, and approval mattered. Learning was by rote or sitting down and copying someone with the knowhow. And since no one wanted to be labelled 'stuck up', they simply got on with it and didn't ask questions. But they were also quick to spot errors and complained about 'mess ups' in everything they did — which they saw as 'keeping up standards'. They were hyper-critical, perhaps because any level of guided activity teaches you just how difficult it is to reach mastery. I learned this as a parent when my son's violin teacher showed him the correct body positions needed to make a good sound.

All this creative energy often seemed to go with eccentricity. So at school we had an English teacher nicknamed 'Dracula' who wore a long black cloak, and an R.E. teacher who set out to terrorise us with Old Testament rants and quotes from Oscar Wilde. At home my ultra-serious dad played Spike Milligan records and quoted Tony Hancock.

Craziness was never far from the surface in such a conformist society, so my family engaged in long-running political arguments, often in deck-chairs on the beach. Also there were numerous taboos, one of which my singing grandpa would break when he was drunk. In front of an audience he'd hold up a lit candle. Then he'd puff and splutter, pretending to have a lip deformity while trying, and failing, to 'blew oot the candle'. This routine, making fun of disabled people, was common at that time in the North East. No one saw how unpleasant it was.

What I see now when I look at photos of my busy family is their drive to stand out. Their stamp albums, knitted hats and record collections were flags to be waved. There was an eagerness and perfectionism about everything they did, a desire to do well and get top marks. They were keen to fit in and yet determined to be different. And they cultivated their own patch as if their lives depended on it.

But my main point is that all these hobbies and activities involved a creative spark. They emphasised the practical and could be messy, but they all took time and effort and stretched people in one way or another. What I think now is that 'being creative' or 'using your talents' isn't necessarily about choosing something with high-art status or being 'up there with the greats'. Creative activity can be everyday and practical and not require an audience. It can be skilful, compassionate, a gift for others, or a personal challenge. The skill's there in everyone. So some people suit caring or listening or working with their hands, and others are better at writing novels.

In my case what I do is both critical, for the record, and an earworm in the head. It's adapted, seen from several angles, and a one-man show. While matching form to content, I'm reinventing language, listening to people and charting feelings. Or to put it another way, in the words of Dylan Thomas: *In my craft and sullen art ... / I labour by singing light / Not for ambition or bread / Or the strut and trade of charms / On the ivory stages / But for the common wages / Of their most secret heart.*

Looked at carefully the spark's always there; it's the writer's job to find it.

# FAMILY ALBUM

I'm holding a photograph album in my hand. Its cover is brown. It has a rough, bobbly, grainy surface, so when it catches the light it looks like snow on a ploughed field. On the left, the double-thickness cardboard is tied by knotted string. On the right, near the bottom, the title 'Photographs' appears faintly in A.L.S. Script. The word is gold and swirly, like an initial page of an illuminated manuscript. Around the edges, the cover has been worn to a smooth, sandy yellow. Its corners are bent.

Before I open it I caution myself. I know what's inside, or I think I know, and I'm wary of my own internal album – the sad backward glance to childhood on the beach, the joke hats and crackers at Christmas parties, the secret battle in the yard to hold the fort against all-comers. I remember my grandpa taking the pictures, pretending the camera had jammed in order to catch people unawares. In my head I can picture his photos of my mum putting out her tongue and my dad chest-out on the beach like a bodybuilder.

When I open the album I see it has four photos to a page. They all have white borders, some faded to grey. Fixed in place by yellowed plastic corners, they show beach-scenes and weddings in black and white, with captions. There are also indoor portraits, couples on doorsteps and groups in parks, people on stations, family snaps by hotels and well-known landmarks, and one or two faded pictures taken of burnt-brown soldiers playing cards in the Western Desert. In the group shots the women wear floral dresses or below-the-knees pleated skirts while the younger men are in shirtsleeves and the older, pipe-smoking men hold hats. Mostly posed, they stand up straight and grin. I'm the short-haired child who appears often at the front of groups. It's as if I'm their mascot.

As I'm looking I'm struck by a thought. All these people, other than my mum and me, are dead. There's a muted sense of absence, a gap between their image and where they are now. They've gone off somewhere, vanished overnight like the family I once knew who packed up and left without saying anything. They're outside life now, in a thinned-out space; but although I feel they're still there I've a sense that I can't touch them. What we shared is in my head – their skin touch and habits, their jokes and teases and what they called their 'ways' – but as a memory, an essence of something — or essence of essence — like a forgotten letter dropped on a pavement, kicked into corners and worn down by the rain.

So all I have is a collection of pictures, each 3" x 4½". They're a gallery of faces, mostly hazy, staring from a distance. The light behind them is thin and watery, and belongs to the past. I can see them as they age, fading into white. Soon they will step out and leave the picture.

Everything I've written stops for this.

# ABOUT LESLIE TATE

## We're in it Together

Sue Hampton
*author of 23 children's books, four adult novels and*
*Ambassador for Alopecia UK*

Leslie and I are *Authors in Love* but even at first glance we're the odd couple too: the long-haired ex-hippie and the bareheaded woman, both of us favouring red except when we choose multi-colour. Our friend, actor-director Mark Crane, calls us #RealGoneCats — which in view of our combined age of 127 delights us no end! But there's more to the straight guy I love than his charity shop waistcoats and look that says 'I could have been a Rolling Stone' because at home my very-male husband wears skirts. And it's not something he's ever been able to tell his mother. Although through our relationship it hasn't been a secret, it hasn't been public knowledge either — because as he explains here in *Heaven's Rage*, there was a time before I knew him when he was outed, cruelly and without principle, by the newspapers. Walking the streets of London in a skirt had always been dangerous; after that traumatic experience he chose self-preservation. Now the time feels right to own his identity as a cross-dressing man, and I'm proud — and moved — to hold his hand.

I met Leslie Stuart Tate on February 20th 2006 in a West End restaurant not far from the National Gallery. But we'd already connected, as a result of Guardian Soulmates, by long and open letter — and we'd spoken, at equal length and with unflinching honesty, on the phone. I was fragile and guilt-ridden after leaving a marriage after 25 years, and I'd told my G.P. that I didn't expect any man to want me. After all, I was a woman with no hair at all and hiding my bald secret under a wig I thought I needed to survive in the world. Not long into our first telephone conversation I explained to the stranger I'd liked at once — but whose face I could only imagine — that I had alopecia. Then I listened. For the pause that I could fill all too easily with the thoughts I ascribed to him. For the embarrassed or even horrified struggle for words. For the burning pan or ring on the doorbell that meant he must rush off. Or even for the click without explanation that ended the call.

'That's interesting,' Leslie said, and admitted he'd never heard of it. That was when he told me he cross-dressed. I knew the term and rather liked Eddie Izzard but that was the sum total of my knowledge and understanding — so we both had a lot to learn. That phone call lasted the best part of an hour; I can picture myself sitting on the carpet of the little flat I was renting, smiling from ear to ear, captivated. I was talking with a man who loved Hughes and Plath, Shakespeare, Dostoevsky ... and Van Gogh, Cezanne and Monet ... and talked about language, feelings, music, the natural world, ballet. A feminist socialist who'd taught like me, but in Secondary and F.E. This was a wise, deep, sensitive and eloquent soul — with a big, abandoned laugh and sense of fun and adventure. Afraid as I was of making a mistake, and doubting as I did my capacity to endure more pain or conflict, I was half in love even before I read the poems he sent me. Without those, I might have called off that meeting in the Indian restaurant. But, read and reread, they confirmed everything I hoped.

Did I have reservations about a man who wore women's clothes? I'd be lying if I claimed none. I would have sworn myself free of prejudice of any kind, but in nearly fifty years I'd only ever counted one (openly) gay human being among my friends. Many years earlier, as a young mum, I'd seen my elderly male neighbour at the window in a bra and I'm ashamed to admit that I told friends as gossip or even a joke. I'd grown up since, but the LGBT community was outside my experience. A friend warned me he would turn out to be gay or bisexual, even if he didn't know it yet. Another told me a story of a cross-dressing colleague with dark, angry psychological problems. Would I have responded, myself, to a lonely heart ad by a cross-dressing man? No. Did I have the thought, 'I just want a normal man'? Well, yes — although I reminded myself of the Jack Nicholson movie *As Good As It Gets*, in which Helen Hunt says the same and her mother tells her, 'Honey, we all do. But there's no such thing.'

You could say everything has changed rather dramatically for both of us since we met that evening, shared our secrets, held hands across the table and knew this was it. I could say I knew even when he walked through the door of the restaurant and I recognised something in the physical presence of him that fleshed out the voice and the poems, and seemed a fit, a match. He wore men's clothes; I wore a wig. Outwardly there was nothing striking or unconventional about us. But what we established by holding nothing back across the table was a trust and an acceptance of each other just as we were. Our histories were different but ridiculous as it sounds, by the time we kissed goodbye at Euston, we both knew we'd taken a bold step towards a shared future. Six weeks later we agreed to move in together — and there really was a double rainbow at the window.

Now, after more than ten years as a couple — tested by health issues including pain and surgery, and the harsh realities of the book business for two full-time writers trying not to lose heart or faith — we've grown closer and stronger. It was with Leslie's encouragement that I first stepped out of our front door without a wig, and I haven't needed or wanted one since because I feel loved, liberated and fully human in my difference. And in the schools I visit as an author, I share the message that we are all of us different in our uniqueness, that our identity lies deeper than hair or clothing, body shape or features, and that diversity enriches our species. We've changed each other. Leslie was an agnostic meat-eater when we met. Now he's vegetarian, I'm vegan and we go to Quaker Meeting and an open-minded, caring church. We belong to the Green Party and abhor the tabloids that incite hatred against those who are 'other' and therefore dismissed as less human than we are. We're both one unit and two extremely different personalities. And I no longer feel any interest in a 'normal' man. In fact, I dispute the whole concept of normality and wish everyone free of its tyranny. In this world we are richly various in every conceivable way. Our survival as a species may depend in part on our ability to unite and address — in climate change, war, the refugee crisis and rampant inequality — much greater problems than any we might find in how others dress, worship or make love.

I love a man who loves me, believes in me and has given me the courage and freedom to be myself. He's gifted, charismatic, funny, intellectual, eccentric, wise, passionate, vivid, ferociously determined and sometimes angry. His flavour is strong, spicy and intense and not to everyone's taste, but nourishes and excites me. I adore and owe him, need him and support him, in all his complexities, flaws and contradictions, in the whole of his soul. Do I fully understand why he needs to dress like a woman? No. But I know that need goes deep in him. I have friends, with hair and with alopecia, who don't fully understand why I choose to go bareheaded in the world. There's no equivalence here but in our different ways we reject exclusive and limited models of masculine and feminine, of what's attractive or acceptable out there, of a one-size, one-style view of humanity. I've believed, since I read those poems before we met, that he's a fine writer with a distinctive and original voice. His novels (two published so far) in the *Lavender Blues trilogy* have inspired me. Now in *Heaven's Rage* he offers an imaginative autobiography exploring imagination, childhood, music and gardens, alcoholism, illness and, yes, cross-dressing. Even in 2016 that takes courage. And I love him for it.

\*\*\*

Leslie wrote his *Lavender Blues* trilogy while attending a University of East Anglia Creative Writing Course. He is a novelist, poet and teacher, with an M.A. in Creative Writing, whose stories are driven by language and character. Leslie admires Virginia Woolf, James Joyce, Carol Shields, Marilynne Robinson and Michael Ondaatje. He runs mixed-arts shows, a poetry reading group and a comedy club, and has led writing workshops at universities, libraries and festivals. He uses music and art as part of his performances which offer surprising insights into prose and how authors 'reread the world'. He often performs with his wife, author Sue Hampton. Calling themselves *Authors in Love*, they live together in Hertfordshire. www.leslietate.com

## BOOKS:
Leslie's trilogy *Lavender Blues: Three Shades of Love* takes us deep into the lives of the Lavender family. The three books, PURPLE, BLUE and VIOLET, explore free love, traditional courtship, open marriage and late-life romance.

## PURPLE
*Purple* is a coming-of-age novel, a portrait of modern love and a family saga. Set in the North of England, it follows the story of shy ingénue Matthew Lavender living through the wildness of the Sixties and his grandmother Mary, born into a traditional working-class family. Both are innocents who have to learn more about long-term love and commitment, earning their independence through a series of revealing and closely-observed relationships.

More details at: http://leslietate.com/shop/purple/ Published Oct 2015.

## BLUE
*Blue* tells the story of Richard and Vanessa Lavender, who join a Nineties feminist collective sharing childcare, political activism and open relationships. Boosted by their 'wider network' they take secondary partners, throw parties and observe the dance of relationships amongst their friends. But finding a balance between power and restraint, and handling shared love, proves difficult ...

*Blue* is the second part of the Lavender Blues trilogy. More details at: http://leslietate.com/shop/blue/ Published Nov 2016.

## VIOLET
Published 2017.

# POSTSCRIPT: A SIX-PART INVENTION


## Follow your Star

The subtitle to *Heaven's Rage* is *Childhood, Survival and Crossing the Gender Line*. I chose the word *Childhood* because that's where it began, writing reflectively about the crazy powers of the untrained mind. I wanted to capture the childhood world I'd lived in — a place full of mystery and repression where unspoken meanings pushed in from all sides. The word *Survival* refers to the sections in the book about alcoholism and illness, but also to the writing about cross-dressing. In all these sections the 'rogue condition' that sets the person apart from society becomes a source of strength. The final phrase, *Crossing the Gender Line*, echoes the 180° rule in film-making[1] i.e. switching gender roles may be confusing, but it's fun — and can be enlightening — when you get used to it!


## The Past is Another Country

If you're like me, when you look back at childhood, the scenes in your mind are set aside, somehow, from the world they were in. There's an abstraction about them, a kind of still life quality that gives them an unreal feel. So it seems that things back then might not have actually happened, and that what we call our past is fragmentary, as if each memory was a dream or a working hypothesis.

---

1 The 180° rule for films states that two characters in a scene should always have the same left/right relationship to each other. Crossing the line happens when the camera moves to the other side of the two characters, reversing their left/right relationship and disorientating the audience.

# Living with Imagination

In *Heaven's Rage* I wanted to describe my early experiences and other formative 'hot spots' and get close to how we *really* remember, which seems to me to be more in discrete cameos than connected narratives. By using different styles I was able to visit and revisit the key moments sampling my experience and focusing on states of being rather than actions, while approaching each incident from more than one angle. And the common thread that ran through all the scenes was the power of the imagination.

# Expression Rules

As I wrote *Heaven's Rage* in parts I found, when I edited it, that I'd sometimes overused the same events. I had to go back and either substitute new material or offer a different viewpoint. As I did so I began to question myself. Was I simply making up a self-justifying version of events? Was I shaping what had happened too much? And was the language driving me to simplify my experiences into a linear narrative, rather than the truth? The answer to all three questions was both yes and no. Words impose order and priorities. Like fiction, they go their own way and won't be fitted to pre-set formulas. Words can also, at times, take you down a tunnel where there's only one way of putting it — usually after repeated edits, and certainly not as you'd intended to write it. So, although I was working from central incidents, a kind of retrospective elaboration crept into my story. And as my autobiography expanded, the themes took over from the personal anecdotes — not a bad thing, because it provided distance and a breathing space for the reflective reader.

# My Imaginary Autobiography

In the end it seemed that the act of writing a so-called factual autobiography had created my own independent, 'fictionalised' life. But the experiences were authentic, and recognisably mine — imaginatively and emotionally, which is how memory works. What we believe happened maybe a construct, but it's true for us, and shapes who we are. There's a stageyness about life, as if we were engaged in continuous attempts at personal reinvention. In *Heaven's Rage* I set out to explore how these pre-conscious beliefs affect our behaviour, so the book examines what you might call the schemas of the heart.

# My Secret Life

We all have impossible dialogues in the head. Being a child while living as an adult was a condition I aimed to recapture in *Heaven's Rage*. Other fantasies such as playing Liszt at the Proms, composing odes while walking in the fields and vaguely-defined spiritual feelings, were all part of the secret-but-oh-so-human experiences that I wanted to share. Because if my book has a lesson for life it is that we all have our personal fables and imaginary audiences. The purpose of *Heaven's Rage* was to own up to these obsessions and to celebrate, with a slightly ironic nod, the stories we all hide in the back of our heads but hesitate to acknowledge.

*Leslie Tate*
*2016*

www.ingramcontent.com/pod-product-compliance
Lightning Source LLC
Chambersburg PA
CBHW060354090426
42734CB00011B/2133